D0466340

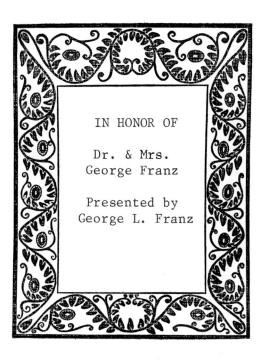

IN HONOR OF

Dr. & Mrs.
George Franz

Presented by
George L. Franz

BENJAMIN WISNER BACON
Pioneer in American Biblical Criticism

by
Roy A. Harrisville

Published by
SCHOLARS PRESS
for
The Society of Biblical Literature

Distributed by

SCHOLARS PRESS
University of Montana
Missoula, Montana 59801

BENJAMIN WISNER BACON

Pioneer in American Biblical Criticism

by

Roy A. Harrisville

Library of Congress Cataloging in Publication Data
Harrisville, Roy A
  Benjamin Wisner Bacon, Pioneer in American Biblical criticism.

  (SBL studies in American Biblical scholarship ; 2)
  Bibliography: p.
  1. Bacon, Benjamin Wisner, 1860-1932. I. Title. II. Series: Society of
Biblical Literature.
SBL studies in American Biblical scholarship ; 2.
BS501.B3H37   220'.092'4 [B]   76-16178
ISBN 0-89130-110-0

Printed in the United States of America

Printing Department
University of Montana
Missoula, Montana 59801

SOCIETY OF BIBLICAL LITERATURE
STUDIES IN AMERICAN BIBLICAL SCHOLARSHIP
SCHOOLS AND SCHOLARS

edited by
Robert W. Funk
and
E. Brooks Holifield

Studies in American Biblical Scholarship 2
Schools and Scholars 2

BENJAMIN WISNER BACON
Pioneer in American Biblical Criticism

by
Roy A. Harrisville

SCHOLARS PRESS
Missoula, Montana

PREFACE

Benjamin Wisner Bacon was not the first to introduce biblical criticism to the United States. That distinction belonged to others, to Moses Stuart or to Bacon's grandfather, Leonard. He did not initiate scholarly study of the Old Testament, no matter how much he deserved to be called a pioneer in the area of documentary criticism, and was not, as is often assumed, the first to author an American introduction to the books of the New Testament.

Yet, Bacon deserves the title "founder" in the area of biblical criticism, because it was he who inaugurated and gave direction to what contemporary scholarship takes for granted as belonging to the curriculum of biblical studies. Whatever work may have been done before him, much of modern American biblical research has the mark of Bacon on it. "Higher critics," those who persist in the conviction that the method appropriate to biblical research is that which deals with the documents from the standpoint of their literary relationships, must acknowledge their debt to Bacon's source analysis and his attendant "appreciation of differences." No serious work on the Gospels of Matthew and John is without its debt to Bacon's *Studies in Matthew* or his *Fourth Gospel in Research and Debate*, which tuned the "higher criticism" to its highest pitch. Even the Jerusalem Bible repeats Bacon's five-fold division of Matthew's Gospel. Those preoccupied with the history of the Gospel forms in the oral, pre-literary stages of their development, will have to concede that Bacon's "aetiological criticism" is a dead ringer for what currently passes for *Formgeschichte*, and that Bacon and no one else was responsible for its introduction to this country, if not for its actual invention. Scholars who are concerned with the liturgical, catechetical and hymnic deposits within the primitive Christian documents must acknowledge Bacon as among the first to concentrate upon the practices of the earliest community as reflected in its literature.

The dust jacket of many a current publication hails its writer as "the author of numerous books and articles on the subject," but no one before and precious few after him have heaped up such a quantity of essays, monographs, reviews, volumes and tomes, and on such a variety of themes, as did Benjamin Bacon. In that respect, there was only one other like him in his generation — Adolf von Harnack. The reason why every candidate of theology or student of religion has heard of Adolf von Harnack, but not of Benjamin Bacon, may have to do with that sudden attack of amnesia from which many suffered in the decade of the Second World War. It was that period which saw the introduction to this country of a "theology of crisis" which ruled out of the discussion queries, hypotheses and conclusions taking their stimulus from an earlier, "liberal" or "modernist" period, and, as was alleged, had more to do with "religion" than with faith. Further, since that theological import had its proper home on the Continent, its popularity led American adherents to assume the truth of the gloss Luther had appended to his edition of the *Theologia Germanica*, viz., "that German theology is best of all." Harnack would be remembered — he was a Continental, and even won new fame by his furnishing a foil for the new passion. If there was any truth in the snide remark of William Sanday, the English divine, to the effect that Bacon, having been to Germany, had "learnt his lesson there too well," there was a kind of irony in the abandonment he and all his tribe had suffered, since Bacon spent little time reading his American contemporaries, and almost all of it ingesting German, French or British opinion. The towering Bacon, who, attired in his varsity sweater loved to watch Eli trounce Harvard at the Bowl, was as teutonic a thinker as a Wellhausen or a Pfleiderer.

Now that the great soloists on the Continent have gone their dusty way to death or retirement, and the patina of familiarity and time has dulled the lustre of a European degree, a new generation, less suggestible and with considerably greater comprehension of its historical origins, is minded to reopen the discussion of questions once tabled or ruled out of order by its predecessors. For this new breed, fascinated with the "classical period of American philosophy," the "classical period of American historiography," the "classical period of American art, etc." Bacon is bound to have relevance, for he belongs to the "classical period of American Bible interpretation."

This volume, beginning with a brief biography of Bacon, proceeds to the description of his advocacy of the "higher criticism" versus fundamentalist "scribalism." It continues with an exposition of his arrangement of the New Testament literature under the rubrics "the Gospel about Jesus," "the Gospel of Jesus" and the "Ephesian synthesis." It then attempts to sketch Bacon's life of Jesus had he lived to write it and concludes with an evaluation which aims at fixing the novel in Bacon's method and at uncovering the spring of his thought.

In light of Bacon's prodigious literary effort, the attempt to integrate his work about a single theme or cluster of themes appeared so huge a task that this volume was postponed for some years. Thanks to the fitful working of the unconscious, the notion suggested itself that the Yale scholar's unremitting struggle with Fundamentalism and his constant accent upon "Spirit" and "freedom" might furnish a focus for that riot of production. Further, the repeated acknowledgement of his debt to Ferdinand Christian Baur, and his contention that the history of primitive Christianity as Baur had constructed it did not require abandoning but only revising, led to that one Continental thinker whose scheme Baur had appropriated, and for whose system "Spirit" and "freedom" furnished the core — G. W. F. Hegel.

I am grateful to the Aid Association to Lutherans, Appleton, Wisconsin, for providing scholarship funds which enabled me to pursue this study apart from teaching duties, and to the Rev. Michael J. Lockerby and Seminarian Christine E. Miller who prepared the footnotes and the typescript.

Roy A. Harrisville
Luther Theological Seminary
St. Paul, Minnesota

CHAPTER ONE
BIOGRAPHICAL BRIEF

Benjamin Wisner Bacon was born on January 15, 1860, at Litchfield, Connecticut, second child and son of Susan (née Bacon) and the Rev. Leonard Woolsey Bacon. Benjamin thus united two Bacon stocks, his father a descendant of Michael who emigrated from Suffolk County, England, in 1636, and his mother a descendant of Nathaniel (the scion of a cousin of Francis Bacon, Lord Verulam) who emigrated from Rutland County, England, in 1656. Of himself Bacon wrote, "Puritanism was thus with me inborn and inbred, every ancestor known to me being of New England Colonial stock."[1]

Educated at private schools in New Haven, Bacon also spent two years at the Coburg Gymnasium, Germany, three at the Collège de Genève, Switzerland, and entered Yale University on September 13, 1877. Bacon's initial choice of a career in medicine evoked little surprise — his clergyman father had earned a degree in medicine and an uncle, Francis, who promised to subsidize the young scholar through medical school, was a practicing physician in New Haven. Awards and scholarships in classical studies, however, convinced Bacon that such capacities as he possessed would be better employed in the ministry.[2] In 1881 he entered the Divinity School of Yale University, due largely to the leadership of his grandfather Leonard, whom he described as the faculty's Nestor.[3] At the end of his career, Bacon described the divinity school as sharing the general hostility to the higher criticism and to the interpretation of biblical concepts in their historical development.[4] Following graduation, Bacon, newly married, and disregarding his father's suggestion of a further year of study at Andover, accepted a unanimous call to a congregation in Old Lyme, Connecticut, where he was ordained and installed June 15, 1884, entering upon his duties July 1.

In the small parish at Lyme, Bacon had leisure for study he had never used during college years. He learned Dutch, entered into correspondence with Abraham Kuenen, and pored over the volumes of W. Robertson Smith, Julius Wellhausen and Otto Pfleiderer. William Rainey Harper, who had left Chicago University for new duties at Yale, learned of Bacon's interest in Pentateuchal criticism and invited him to participate in his graduate seminars. Harper assigned Bacon a part in his controversy with William Henry Green of Princeton over the documentary analysis of the Pentateuch, the results published in *Hebraica*, Harper's newly founded journal.[5]

In 1888, Bacon moved to his second and last parish in Oswego, New York. While there he attempted in book form to give graphic illustration of the consensus of modern scholarship regarding Pentateuchal analysis,[6] and wrestled with the question of the Hebrew calendar.[7]

In recognition of his early researches, Bacon's alma mater granted him an honorary M.A. degree in the spring of 1892, and in the year following Western Reserve University conferred on him the doctor's degree *honoris causa*. In this period, he became a member of the Society of Biblical Literature and Exegesis which, as he put it, became the "unfailing recipient" of his contributions for over forty years. Bacon himself presided over the Society in 1902-03, and functioned as its managing editor from 1907-08. The year 1894 saw Bacon's second published volume,[8] prepared for by a series of articles in *Hebraica*.[9] Bacon stated that with this volume, with his translation of Karl Budde's notes on the books of Samuel and G. Wildeboer's study of the Old Testament canon,[10] his essays on Old Testament criticism came to an end. He nonetheless continued sporadically to discourse on Old Testament themes as late as 1904.[11] At any rate, the commencement of Bacon's New Testament studies was signalled in a twelve-page article entitled "The Displacement of John 14," published in 1894.[12]

Though Bacon spoke of his linguistic shortcomings as influencing his choice of the New Testament as a field of specialization, he referred to an invitation from Syracuse

University in 1895 to deliver a course of biblical lectures as leading indirectly to the most decisive step in his career.[13] Upon the transfer of Prof. George B. Stevens from the chair of New Testament to that of Systematic Theology in 1896, Bacon applied for candidacy to the New Testament post at Yale. Prof. George P. Fisher, College Pastor, Professor of Divinity, and preacher at Bacon's ordination, so feared Bacon would destroy the school with his radical views that a tenured position appeared impossible. At the suggestion of Delia Lyman Porter, wife of Bacon's lifetime friend and colleague, he announced his willingness to come for a trial year.[14] At the end of Bacon's probation in 1897, he succeeded to tenure as Buckingham Professor of New Testament Criticism and Interpretation.

The summer following his probationary year, Bacon left for Europe where he was a guest of Otto Pfleiderer at Gross Lichterfeld; met Bernard and Johannes Weiss at Berlin and Marburg; Willibald Beyschlag and Erich Haupt at Jena; Budde and H. J. Holtzmann at Strassburg; Stade and Bertholet in Giessen; Wernle at Zürich; Jülicher at Marburg and Wellhausen at Göttingen — visits which he described as having to "take the place of years of academic preparation."[15]

During his entire tenure, Bacon took two leaves of absence. The first (1905-06) was spent at the American School of Oriental Research in Jerusalem, where he served as resident director. During this period he toured the Syrian sun-temples near Baalbek; stopped at Bethlehem over Christmas; discovered a new inscription from upper Galilee and inspected the locality of the ancient Betanim-Batnia-Bataneas. In 1928, through Bacon's mediation, Yale received a commission from the British government to excavate part of the ancient city of Gerasa, site of the narrative in Mark 5:1-20, in cooperation with the British School of Archaeology.[16] On his second leave (1920-21), Bacon was invited to deliver the Hibbard Lectures at Manchester College, Oxford. Following Michaelmas term there, he travelled across Europe to meet Sir William M. Ramsey at Constantinople, returning later to England to lecture at

Oxford's summer school of theology. Prior to this second leave, Bacon had spent the summer at the *Weltkongress für freies Christentum und religiösen Fortschritt* and at a comparable though smaller gathering in Pontigny, France, convened by Paul Desjardins and Alfred Loisy.[17]

Bacon received a host of degrees, though all were honorary. In addition to those noted above he received a Litt.D. from Syracuse in 1895; an LL.D. from Illinois College in 1904; a Th.D. from Breslau in 1911; an S.T.D. from Harvard in 1914 and a Litt.D. from Oxford in 1920. Reflecting on the risk Yale had run by admitting a fledgling with minimal credentials to an exceptionally important chair, Bacon stated that he would have been incapable of successfully sustaining a Yale Ph.D. examination. In 1928 he retired at the prescribed age of sixty-eight, concluding a thirty-six year career. The year following, Yale invited its professor emeritus to deliver the inaugural series of Kent Shaffer Lectures, published in 1930 under the title *Jesus The Son of God*.[18] On Monday, February 1, 1932, in apparently good health, Bacon died suddenly of a heart attack at the age of seventy-two years, and was buried in Grove Street Cemetery, New Haven.

---

1. "Enter the Higher Criticism," *Contemporary American Theology*, Theological Autobiographies, ed. Vergilius Ferm (New York: Round Table Press, 1932), I, 18f.
2. *A History of The Class of 'Eighty-One*, Yale College (New York: The Trow Press, 1909), II, 40.
3. Bacon's grandfather was a graduate of Yale College and Andover Seminary, the pastor of Center Church, New Haven, from 1825 to 1866. He served as Acting Professor of Revealed Theology at the Divinity School from 1866 to 1871, and from then till his death in 1881 was Lecturer in Ecclesiastical Polity and American Church History. When the Old Testament scholar W. Robertson Smith had been dismissed from his chair at Aberdeen, Scotland, because of his advocacy of the German "higher criticism," it was Leonard Bacon who proposed that he be invited to lecture at the Divinity School.
4. "Enter the Higher Criticism," p. 17; "Royce's Interpretation of Christianity," *PhilosophicalReview*, XXV (1916), p. 320.
5. "Pentateuchal Analysis I," *Hebraica*, IV (1888), pp. 216-43; "Pentateuchal Analysis II," *Hebraica*, V (1888), pp. 7-17; "Notes on the Analysis of Genesis xv," *Hebraica*, VII (1890), p. 75f.; "Notes on

the Analysis of Genesis i.-xxxi," *Hebraica*, VII (1891), pp. 222-31; "Notes on the Analysis of Genesis xxxii.-1," *Hebraica*, VII (1891), pp. 278-88; "The Blessing of Isaac, Genesis xxvii. — A Study in Pentateuchal Analysis," *Hebraica*, VII (1891), pp. 143-48.

6. *The Genesis of Genesis*: A Study of the Documentary Sources of the First Book of Moses in accordance with the Results of Critical Science Illustrating the Presence of Bibles within the Bible (Hartford: The Student Publishing Company, 1893).

7. "Chronology of the Account of the Flood in P. — A Contribution to the History of the Jewish Calendar," *Hebraica*,VIII (1892), pp. 79-88; "The Calendar of Enoch and Jubilees," *Hebraica*, VIII (1892), pp. 124-31.

8. *The Triple Tradition of the Exodus*. A Study of the Structure of the later Pentateuchal Books, reproducing the Sources of the Narrative, and further illustrating the Presence of Bibles within the Bible (Hartford: The Student Publishing Company, 1894).

9. "JE in the Middle Books of the Pentateuch. I. Analysis of Exodus vii.-xii," *Journal of Biblical Literature*, IX (1890), pp. 161-200; "JE in the Middle Books of the Pentateuch. III. Analysis of Exodus xii.37-xvii.16," *Journal of Biblical Literature*, XI (1892), pp. 177-200; "JE in the Middle Books of the Pentateuch. IV. Sinai-Horeb: Analysis of Exodus xviii.-xxxiv," *Journal of Biblical Literature*, XII (1893), pp. 23-46.

10. G. Wildeboer, *The Origin of the Canon of the Old Testament*, trans. B. W. Bacon (London: Luzac and Company, 1895). The preface to this volume was written by George Foote Moore who stated that the translator's own contribution to the criticism of the Old Testament had earned him "a good name among scholars."

11. "Solomon in Tradition and in Fact," *The New World*, VII (1898), pp. 212-28; "Abraham the Heir of Yahweh," *The New World*, VIII (1899), pp. 674-90; "Was Saul a Hashish-Eater?" *The Expository Times*, XV (1904), p. 380.

12. *Journal of Biblical Literature*, XIII (1894).

13. "Enter the Higher Criticism," pp. 25, 32.

14. Roland Bainton, *Yale and the Ministry* (New York: Harper and Brothers, 1957), p. 181f.

15. "Enter the Higher Criticism," pp. 36ff.

16. The following reflect Bacon's archaeological activity during this period: "Among the Sun Temples of Coele-Syria," *Records of the Past*, V (1906), pp. 67-83; "Christmas in Bethlehem," *The Independent*, LXI (1906), pp. 1459-463; "The Institute of Archaeology in Jerusalem," *Yale Divinity Quarterly*, II (1906), pp. 124-28; "A New Inscription from Upper Galilee," *The American Journal of Archaeology*, XI (1907), pp. 315-20; "The Baptism of John — Where was It?" *The Biblical World*, XXX (1907), pp. 39-50; "Eagle and Basket on the Antioch Chalice," *Annual of the American Schools of Oriental Research*, V (1925), pp. 1-22.

17. "A Summer among Modernists," *The Independent*, LXIX (1910), pp. 1208-212.

18. New York: Henry Holt and Company, 1930.

CHAPTER TWO
ENTER THE HIGHER CRITICISM

I: *The Crisis in Authority and the Fundamentalist Reaction*:

Toward the end of his career Bacon wrote:

> So far as my life-work has contributed to the development of
> theology in America it has been through securing to the methods
> and results of the higher criticism their rightful place in the
> progressive work of Reformers, Puritans, and New England
> divines. An account of my individual relation to the progress of
> theology in America . . . must center upon the coming in of this
> "era of the so-called higher criticism."[1]

Bacon acknowledged that the area of his concentration
was only the salient of a larger front, that of the crisis in
authority and education confronting the Protestant world of
his time.[2] Bacon saw clear evidence of the crisis in what he
lauded as the "dangerous younger generation's" substitution
of an "experiential authority" for the authority of dogma.[3]
At the same time, he had anxious eyes for the educational
crisis as reflected in the irreligion prevalent in American
institutions of higher learning and in the church's failure to
provide genuine religious instruction.[4]

If the crisis in authority and education provided the
context for Bacon's life-work, its immediate occasion was a
reaction to a phenomenon which Bacon both scorned and
feared — Fundamentalism. According to him, Fundamentalism constituted the attempt to identify Christianity
with the particular form it had assumed at a given time[5] and
assumed concrete shape in what he termed a rabbinic,
scribal, post-Reformation dogma or tradition about the
Bible.[6]

To Bacon's mind, the means by which Fundamentalism
attempted to meet the current crisis were twofold. The first
he described as the imposition of the "mortmain" of creeds.

New England Congregationalism had resorted to such imposition when, faced with a robust intellectual liberalism, it had attempted to counter it by drafting creeds as tests of faith.[7] The second technique Bacon described as the establishment of the theological "seminary." In their zeal for conforming to the "instruments" of the various denominations, theological schools had broken away from universities to place themselves under sectarian standards.[8]

For Bacon, the results of the Fundamentalist reaction were dire in the extreme. Fundamentalism spelled repression in the matter of biblical interpretation, and its imposition of creeds constituted such a barrier to learning and scholarly productivity as to render merely the German universities capable of turning out the great texts in theology and of leading the theological thought of the world.[9] Bacon further referred to the Fundamentalist reaction as spawning a class of the partly informed.[10] The attempt to delay the introduction of a science over one hundred years old rendered not only clergy and lay but also a considerable number of scholars ignorant of the higher criticism.[11]

Bacon was not without admiration for certain members of the Fundamentalist school. He wrote, for example, of Theodor Zahn's *Einleitung in das Neue Testament*, that if it were the last word in critical science the situation would be discouraging indeed, yet spoke of it as an indispensable text-book of conservatism and described it as a marvel of learning and skill.[12] Bacon nevertheless reserved his bitterest prose for Fundamentalism, characterizing it as a type of governmental authority which appealed to fear[13] and which represented a "sophomoric stage of appreciation" in biblical matters.[14] In short, it was a "blind, pathetic protest" which had brought theology into disrepute and was in danger of drawing down upon itself and the cause it championed the contempt and ridicule of the cultured world.[15] But with all his scorn for Fundamentalism, Bacon was unwilling to acquit the broader Church of complicity in the reaction. Since it fell to the clergy to enlighten the laity, and since the gulf between the scholar's and ordinary reader's understanding lay at the door of the Church's improper

education of its clergy, the broader Church had aided and
abetted the reaction.[16]

The means Bacon proposed to thwart the
Fundamentalist threat were two-fold. First, he opposed to
Fundamentalism's use of creeds as tests their use as
"testimonies" or forms of worship.[17] Second, to
Fundamentalism's "seminary" concept, Bacon opposed the
return of the Scriptures to their legitimate place in the
schools, contending that the scientific study of Christianity
was essential not only to clergy and laity, but to every man of
culture.[18] On the other hand, he regarded the reintroduction
of religious education in the American public schools as
unlikely, and set his hope for genuine religious education in
the university divinity school.[19] The degree of Bacon's
confidence in theological instruction's producing a
"competent and burning herald"[20] is reflected in the signal
role he assigned to Yale. According to him, it was Yale which
had conceived its unique role among institutions of learning
as fostering "the true spirit of free and fearless pursuit of
religious truth."[21] To this free and fearless pursuit under the
elder Dwight, Bacon attributed Unitarianism's lack of
headway and Connecticut's avoidance of the schism of "old"
and "new" schools which had rent Congregationalism in
Massachusetts.[22] To Dwight's son, Timothy the younger,
Bacon credited the theological school's deliverance from
near extinction following the Civil War.[23]

Throughout his career, Bacon took pride in Yale's
having escaped the divorce between divinity school and
university which Harvard, Union and Princeton had
suffered. For him it was no small contribution to the cause of
theological education to "prove experimentally" what it
means that a divinity school should remain an integral part
of the university's life.[24] Alien to the "seminary" idea,
Puritans had set church and schoolhouse side by side.

II. *Bacon's Presuppositions*:

That which distanced Bacon in a material way from the
Fundamentalist reaction was his insistence upon a "rational

and scientific conception of the process and history from which the religious and spiritual consciousness of Christendom has issued."[25] History, for Bacon, constituted a process of which the whole, and not any single stage, was of the essence.[26] Contending that immanence, continuity and uniformity were the mark of the divine,[27] he stated that the revelation of the divine will could be read from out of "natural law."[28] At the base of "natural law" lay an intelligible process containing "just as much of God" as the idea of the supernatural.[29] Bacon thus described miracle as an unusual event occurring in accord with laws not yet understood[30] and credited the notion of miracle as intervention to the biblical writer's account and not to the event itself. Thus, he concluded, the miraculous had lost its evidential character.

For Bacon, the idea of a God active within the historical process as a whole implied some notion of evolution.[31] Not, however, of biological evolution, since he believed such a development had already reached its *telos*.[32] Life, history was now to be conceived in terms of a "spiritual evolution."[33] Though he naturally referred to that "Power" immanent in the historical process as "God," the term by which he preferred to signalize the entirety of the divine activity was that of "Spirit." Bacon hence defined biblical criticism as a "phenomenology of the Spirit," a "spiritual biology," and the Bible a "collection of living specimens."[34] By disentangling primitive thread from the web of pious legend in order to arrive at the "plain, bald facts, just the events as they occurred,"[35] biblical criticism would dissolve every authority but that of the Spirit with which men were to be left alone.[36] Positively, the task of criticism was to rebuild the literature of the primitive church into an ordered whole,[37] since, as Bacon put it, "the whole, and only the whole, is the Logos of God."[38]

This type of criticism, according to Bacon, involved distinguishing the "eternal principle" or "essence" from what is local, temporary or belonging to the "garment."[39] It involved singling out that "vitalizing germ or dynamic of growth" which enabled the religion of Jesus to assimilate all the worthy elements of Jewish and Hellenistic religious life from Paul's day to our own.[40] It would lead to the knowledge of "man as he will be when the Power that informs the material creation with spiritual content has accomplished its design,"[41] and since "man" partook of the Logos as process, "the man that is to be . . . is the revealer, the Logos of God."[42]

For Bacon, religious phenomena outside the history of Judaism and Christianity belonged to that "whole." For that reason, biblical criticism enjoyed an essential relation to other sciences involved in the "phenomenology of Spirit,"[43] and was thus sister to the History of Religions School.[44]

III. *Bacon's Method*:

The method which Bacon believed most appropriate to the critical task was, of course, the genetic.[45] Stating that the "emphasis on literary dissection" had been misplaced, he heaped scorn on the "grasshopper exegete,"[46] and opposed to such narrowness "thinking the thoughts" of the biblical writer,[47] that is, by inquiry into the documents deriving a theory of the context in which the writer's ideas were moulded.[48]

If, for Bacon, mere documentary analysis was not up to the biblical-critical task, he did not disparage its use, but employed it to the full, and on at least one occasion termed it the critic's "prior interest."[49] But in keeping with his commitment to the method of the History of Religions School, he sought to give larger scope to documentary research by what he termed an "appreciation of differences." Bacon stated that in order to apprehend a truth presented under various aspects, it was necessary to measure the distance between its observers or recorders, and from this base line measure the angles toward the original point of divergence.[50] Thus, in order to glean the true nature of Pauline versus Petrine thought, Bacon compared Galatians with Acts.[51] For the nature and sequence of the Second Synoptic Source or "S" he compared Matthew and Mark.[52] In order to derive a picture of the nature and design of "Q"

Bacon removed the Markan element from Matthew after allowing for Mark's influence on the order of Matthew, and compared the remainder with the form and order it had received in Luke.[53]

The method, however, for which Bacon is most celebrated is what he called the "aetiological."[54] First coined by Menzies in his *The Earliest Gospel,*[55] Bacon described the method as "the effort retrospectively to account for and justify existing practices and beliefs" as reflected in the Gospel narratives.[56] He contended that the Gospels were "aetiological narratives" which purported to give an account of Christian origins,[57] and as a result, any Gospel which tradition and internal evidence could concur in exhibiting as *the* Gospel of one of the great provinces of the apostolic church reflected in its structure the interpretation of Christianity characteristic of that region.[58] This "reflection" Bacon termed the "theory of pragmatic values,"[59] writing that the original evangelic tradition did not consist of biographies or books, but of loosely connected anecdotes strung together for the purpose of explaining or defending beliefs and practices of the contemporary church.[60]

Adolf von Harnack's hearty endorsement of Bacon's method[61] is suggestive of its originality. It was not, of course, without antecedents. Bacon spoke of his applying to Gospel criticism the same principle which the Graf-Kuenen school had applied to the historical tradition of the Old Testament,[62] and suggested that he was led naturally to the method by having begun his studies with an investigation of the narrative books of the Old Testament in which the ancient story so frequently concludes with a "therefore" — "therefore a man leaves his father and his mother and cleaves to his wife."[63] Of the various methods Bacon used, that of aetiological criticism received the greater attention.

As supplement, Bacon employed what he called the "method of implication" or conjecture.[64] He wrote that under appropriate safeguards sufficient to exclude unwarranted inferences and subjective fancy, conjecture was an admissible tool. Indeed, historical research would lack creative power without it,[65] since in face of certain tasks no other method lay ready to hand.

From the standpoint of method and presuppositions, the scholar of whom Bacon gave clearest reminder was Ferdinand Christian Baur. Acknowledging that Baur had taught a truly historical appreciation of the New Testament books,[66] he reckoned that the great German scholar had not gotten his due,[67] though with him system had finally prevailed over chaos.[68] To Bacon's mind, Baur's theory was of permanent validity on two counts: First, because it concerned itself with the history of the Christian ideas as embodied in its literature,[69] and second because it required that the issues of primitive Christianity be defined by way of scrutinizing the epistles of Paul.[70] For these reasons, then, Baur's outline required correction, not disproof.[71] Its beginning point, viz., the division of the Christian mission into a Petrine apostolate of the circumcision and a Pauline apostolate of the Gentiles retained its validity.[72] "Thesis" and "antithesis" were thus present from the very beginning.[73] At the same time, Bacon stated that the gospel's translation from Jewish to Greek soil was deeper and more complex than Baur had conceived.[74] Contending that current criticism was in a better position than Baur to reconstruct the situation in the primitive community, Bacon called for a reduction of the period of Baur's formula,[75] asserting that the reconciliation in catholicity which the Tübingen critic had fixed for the age of Justin and Irenaeus had already begun with Paul himself.[76]

Bacon did not assume that research construed as inquiry into the "plain, bald facts" would yield a formula of supreme authority. Criticism was subject to change, whereas matters of faith could not be.[77] Writing of the limitations of criticism anent the Life-of-Jesus Research, he stated that

> every source of criticism may well be applied to the recovery of the last crumb of Jesus' teaching, the last fragment of trustworthy testimony to his character and career. But unless with Paul and Mark we see in this career the hand of God, we too have abdicated our rightful task as theologians. . . . Criticism without theology,

handing back to us the empty shell of evolutionary processes instead of the divine work of Redemption . . . may well provoke indignant reaction.[78]

Thus, Bacon was led to distinguish two "Gospels" within the literature of the primitive Christian community, the one the "Gospel of" and the other the "Gospel about Jesus," nomenclature for which he was dependent upon von Harnack, whose lecture on "The Religion of Jesus, and the Religion about Jesus" he had heard in Berlin in 1913.[79]

To the "Gospel of Jesus" corresponded the "Quest" for the historical Jesus as "representative of the divine idea," the "phenomenon of the life of God in man and man in God,"[80] in short the extricating of Jesus' moral and religious teaching from the web of "pious legend."[81] In face of the scepticism of Albert Schweitzer, Bacon asserted that the "facts" were a part of the scholar's inquiry, and gave the lie to the notion that Christianity had nothing else upon which to build than the "Christ-idea."[82] Yet, Bacon's seemingly sanguine view of the possibilities of a "Quest" was diminished by his assertion that its goal lay not in a physical portrait, but in a "portrait of the character of Jesus,"[83] of his "consciousness of filial relation to God."[84]

To the "Gospel about Jesus" corresponded the other, more important aspect of the scholar's inquiry, viz., the interpretation of legendary or mythological elements in the New Testament. Bacon asserted that "our business is to interpret legend, not to cast it out,"[85] and condemned liberalism's elimination of the mythological.[86] Historical appreciation of the value of the mythological thus paved the way for a "more rational view." It constituted a "forerunner" of a more "philosophic" estimate of Jesus' life and death as representing the divine idea.[87]

These two components, Bacon contended, the "Gospel of" and the "Gospel about Jesus," or, the outward fact as pursued by the Ritschlian School and the inner experience of it as elucidated by Schleiermacher, were blended in the primitive Christian community from Pentecost onward. The adjustment of the two constituted the issue in the controversy between Paul and the Galilean apostles,[88] and to this adjustment Bacon devoted the study of a life-time.

---

1. "Enter the Higher Criticism," pp. 1, 5.
2. "The Problem of Religious Education and the Divinity School," *The American Journal of Theology*, VIII (1904), p. 687.
3. "The Decline of Moral Authority," *Yale Review*, XVII (1928), pp. 310, 313, 318.
4. "The Teaching Ministry for To-Morrow, *The Centennial Celebration of the Yale Divinity School* (New Haven: Yale University Press, 1922), p. 12f.; "Fundamentalism in America," *The Expository Times*, XXXV (1924), p. 314.
5. "The Contribution of Newman Smyth to Theology," *Recollections and Reflections*, ed. Newman Smyth (New York: Charles Scribner's Sons, 1926), p. 229.
6. "The New Theology," *Church Union* (January, 1898), p. 362; *The Triple Tradition of the Exodus*, p. 71; "Right and Wrong Use of the Bible," *The Congregationalist*, CX (1925), p. 392f.; "Die Ergebnisse der Bibelkritik für Theologie und Praxis," *Sonderausgabe aus dem Protokoll des 5. Weltkongresses für Freies Christentum und Religiösen Fortschritt* (Berlin-Schöneberg: Protestantischer Schriftenvertrieb, 1911), p. 4.
7. Cf. *Theodore Thornton Munger, New England Minister* (New Haven: Yale University Press, 1913), pp. 164, 192f. Bacon saw this imposition also reflected in the Protestant Episcopal Church's attempt to change its name to the "Holy Catholic Church of America," thus arrogating to itself a title rightfully deserved by "ninety-nine of one hundred Protestant Christians of the more thoughtful and earnest type," cf. "Protestant Episcopal or Holy Catholic?" *The Independent*, LXXIV (1913), p. 908f.
8. "Fundamentalism in America," p. 314.
9. "The Problem of Religious Education and the Divinity School," p. 693.
10. "Are the Critics Come to Canossa?" *The Outlook*, LVI (1897), p. 120.
11. "Bible Instruction in Colleges," *The Forum*, IX (1890), p. 304f.
12. A review of Theodor Zahn's *Einleitung in das Neue Testament*, Band II, *The American Journal of Theology*, V (1901), p. 557.
13. "The Problem of Religious Education and the Divinity School," pp. 684ff.
14. "Ultimate Problems of Biblical Science," *Journal of Biblical Literature*, XXII (1903), p. 11.
15. "The Teaching Ministry for To-Morrow," p. 16f.

16. "Bible Instruction in Colleges," p. 307; "Punctuation, Translation, Interpretation," *The Journal of Religion*, IV (1924), p. 243; cf. "The Problem of Religious Education and the Divinity School," p. 691.

17. While at Oswego, Bacon wrote an explanation of the form of admission to membership in his parish. Application by letter or confession should be made to the congregation's "Prudential Committee," and announced from the pulpit one week prior to Communion. The applicant should then become a member by vote at the "lecture" preparatory to Communion, or by uniting on confession after the rite of baptism or confirmation. The confession or "Articles of Belief" to which the candidate was to give verbal assent offered the "largest measure of sympathy in religious belief to Christians of all denominations," but might be replaced by forms more acceptable to the candidate. Following his confession, the candidate would then strike a mutual agreement with the congregation under the "covenant" rubric, the service concluding with the administration of the Sacrament. Cf. "How to Join the Church and Why," An Explanation of the Form of Admission to Membership of the Congregational Church of Oswego, New York, with a Brief Summary of Reasons for an avowed Loyalty to the Kingdom of Christ (Oswego, New York: Printed by the Church, 1893), pp. 5-7, 9, 14, 16.

18. "Bible Instruction in Colleges," pp. 300-02.

19. "The Problem of Religious Education and the Divinity School," p. 692.

20. "The Teaching Opportunity of the Pulpit," *The Church School Journal*, LIX (1927), p. 65.

21. "The Theological Significance of Jonathan Edwards," Proceedings at the Dedication of the Memorial Gateway to Jonathan Edwards at the Old Burning Ground, South Windsor, June 25, 1929 (By the Connecticut Society of the Colonial Dames of America), p. 23.

22. "The Development of the School and Its Contributions to Theological Education," *Yale Alumni Weekly* (October 20, 1922), p. 117.

23. "Timothy Dwight's Life-Work for Yale," *Yale Alumni Weekly Supplement*, XXVI (1917), pp. 13, 17, 19f.

24. "The Development of the School and Its Contributions to Theological Education," p. 118.

25. "Bible Instruction in Colleges," p. 302.

26. *He Opened To Us The Scriptures* (New York: The Macmillan Co., 1923), p. 64.

27. "The New Theology," p. 361.

28. "Does It Pay the Modern Man to Pray?" *The Congregationalist*, XC (1905), p. 280.

29. *Jesus and Paul* (New York: The Macmillan Co., 1921), p. 80.

30. "The New Theology," p. 361; *The Story of St. Paul* (New York: Houghton, Mifflin and Co., 1904), p. 51f.

31. *Christianity Old and New* (New Haven: Yale University Press, 1914), p. 27.

32. "Ultimate Problems of Biblical Science," p. 2.
33. Ibid., p. 1.
34. "Die Ergebnisse der Bibelkritik für Theologie und Praxis," p. 11; "Criticism and the Church," *The Outlook*, LXXIX (1905), p. 239.
35. "Ultimate Problems of Biblical Science," p. 13.
36. "Die Ergebnisse der Bibelkritik für Theologie und Praxis," p. 10.
37. "A Century of Change in New Testament Criticism," *The Hibbert Journal*, XI (1913), p. 612.
38. "Ultimate Problems of Biblical Science," p. 4.
39. "The Exegesis of Tomorrow," *The Outlook*, LXVII (1901), p. 72.
40. "Criticism and the Church," p. 241.
41. "Ultimate Problems of Biblical Science," p. 1.
42. *Ibid.*; cf. "The Mythical Collapse of Historical Christianity," *The Hibbert Journal*, IX (1911), p. 753.
43. "The Relations of New Testament Science to Kindred Sciences," *Congress of Arts and Science*, Universal Exposition, St. Louis, 1904, ed. Howard J. Rogers (Boston: Houghton, Mifflin and Co., 1906), II, 571.
44. *Ibid.*, p. 571f.; cf. *He Opened To Us The Scriptures*, p. 58. Bacon frequently and passionately hailed the advent and ascendancy of this school, and took particular pride in the fact that Harvard had created a meeting-point for its two departments of religious literature and divinity in a new chair of The History of Religions, and in that chair had "wisely placed" a Yale man, "the foremost biblical scholar of America," George Foote Moore. Cf. "The Exegesis of Tomorrow," p. 71; "The Mythical Collapse of Historical Christianity," p. 742f.; "The Relations of New Testament Science to Kindred Sciences," p. 572.
45. The Exegesis of Tomorrow," p. 71; "Die Ergebnisse der Bibelkritik für Theologie und Praxis," p. 12; "Jewish Interpretations of the New Testament," *The American Journal of Theology*, XIX (1915), p. 167; "Historico-Critical Analysis of the Book of Acts," Abstract of Lectures to the Students of Yale Divinity School (New Haven: Raven Press, n.d.), p. 12.
46. "The Exegesis of Tomorrow," p. 68.
47. "Ultimate Problems of Biblical Science," p. 10.
48. *The Triple Tradition of the Exodus*, p. xvii; "The Exegesis of Tomorrow," p. 67; "Primitive Christianity," review of Otto Pfleiderer's *Das Urchristentum*, *The American Journal of Theology*, VII (1903), p. 770; "Criticism and the Church," p. 239; *He Opened To Us The Scriptures*, p. 116.
49. *Studies in Matthew*, p. 120; cf. "Some 'Western' Variants in the Text of Acts," *The Harvard Theological Review*, XXI (1928), p. 118.
50. "Historico-Critical Analysis of the Book of Acts," p. 12f.
51. "Acts versus Galatians: The Crux of Apostolic History," *The American Journal of Theology*, XI (1907), especially pp. 454, 474; *The Story of St. Paul*, pp. 82, 99; *Commentary on the Epistle of Paul to the Galatians* (New York: The Macmillan Co., 1909), pp. 32, 38, 125.

52. "The Order of the Lukan 'Interpolations.' II. The Smaller Interpolation," *Journal of Biblical Literature*, XXXVI (1917), p. 125.

53. "The Nature and Design of Q, the Second Synoptic Source," The Hibbert Journal, xxii (1924), p. 680.

54. "Gospel Types in Primitive Tradition," *The Hibbert Journal*, IV (1906), p. 878; "Jesus Christ," *The New Schaff-Herzog Encyclopedia of Religious Knowledge* (New York: Funk and Wagnalls, 1910), VI, 160f.; "The Purpose of Mark's Gospel," *Journal of Biblical Literature*, XXIX (1910), p. 43.

55. "A Turning Point in Synoptic Criticism," *The Harvard Theological Review*, I (1908), p. 66, n. 54.

56. "The Purpose of Mark's Gospel," p. 43.

57. "Jesus Christ," p. 160.

58. "Gospel Types in Primitive Tradition," p. 879f.

59. *The Beginnings of Gospel Story*, A Historical-Critical Inquiry into the Sources and Structure of the Gospel according to Mark (New Haven: Yale University Press, 1909), p. ix; "The Purpose of Mark's Gospel," pp. 41, 49; "The Resurrection in Primitive Tradition and Observance," *The American Journal of Theology*, XV (1911), p. 374.

60. *The Beginnings of Gospel Story*, p. ix; "The Purpose of Mark's Gospel," pp. 41, 44.

61. "Sie haben in ihr ein Gedanken zum Leitstern gemacht der gewiss richtig ist," quoted in "The Resurrection in Primitive Tradition and Observance," p. 374.

62. *The Beginnings of Gospel Story*, p. ix.

63. "The Purpose of Mark's Gospel," p. 43.

64. "The Q Section on John the Baptist and the Shemoneh Esreh," *Journal of Biblical Literature*, XLV (1926), p. 34.

65. "Andronicus," *The Expository Times*, XLII (1931), p. 304.

66. *An Introduction to the New Testament* (New York: Macmillan and Co., 1900), p. 18. For many months, ill health interrupted work on the *Introduction*, and his colleague Frank Porter took down at dictation the last chapter from Bacon's sick bed.

67. "Ferdinand Christian Baur," *Actes du IVᵉ Congres International d'Histoire des Religions, Tenu à Leide du 9ᵉ-13ᵉ Septembre* (Leiden: E. J. Brill, 1913), p.156.

68. "A Century of Change in New Testament Criticism," p. 612.

69. *The Making of the New Testament* (London: Williams and Norgate, 1912), p. 41.

70. "A Turning Point in Synoptic Criticism," p. 65.

71. *The Making of the New Testament*, pp. 45, 47.

72. *Is Mark a Roman Gospel?*, Harvard Theological Studies, VII (Cambridge: Harvard University Press, 1919), p. 105.

73. *The Making of the New Testament*, p. 40.

74. *Ibid.*, p. 42.

75. "The Leiden Congress for the History of Religions," *The American*

Journal of Theology, XVII (1913), p. 156; "Historico-Critical Analysis of the Book of Acts," p. 12; *The Making of the New Testament*, p. 45.

76. *Is Mark a Roman Gospel?* p. 105; cf. p. 22 below.

77. "The Supernatural Birth of Jesus: I. Can it be established historically?" *The American Journal of Theology* , X (1906), p. 2f.; cf. "The Jesus of History and the Christ of Religion. The Approach toward Consistency," *Jesus or Christ? The Hibbert Journal Supplement* (London: Williams and Norgate, 1909), p. 221; "Miracle and Scripture," *The Modern Churchman*, X (1920), pp. 287, 295; "The Return to Theology," *Christianity and Modern Thought*, ed. Ralph H. Gabriel (New Haven: Yale University Press, 1924), p. 122f.

78. "The Success and Failure of Liberalism," *Yale Review*, XIII (1923), p. 96.

79. *The Story of Jesus and the Beginnings of the Church*, A Valuation of the Synoptic Record for History and for Religion (New York: The Century Co., 1927), p. 9f.

80. "The Jesus of History and the Christ of Religion," pp. 209, 223; *The Fourth Gospel in Research and Debate* (New Haven: Yale University Press, 1910), p. 533; *Christianity Old and New*, p. 39.

81. "Ultimate Problems of Biblical Science," p. 13; "Reading the Gospels Backward," *The Hibbert Journal*, XXX (1931-1932), p. 89.

82. *Christianity Old and New*, p. 122; "The Institute of Archaeology in Jerusalem," pp. 124, 126; "The Return to Theology," p. 123; "Die Ergebnisse der Bibelkritik für Theologie und Praxis," p. 11; "The Mythical Collapse of Historical Christianity," p. 749.

83. *Christianity Old and New*, p. 131f.

84. "Ultimate Problems of Biblical Science," p. 14.

85. "The Mythical Collapse of Historical Christianity," p. 744.

86. *The Story of Jesus and the Beginnings of the Church*, pp. 5, 19; "The Success and Failure of Liberalism," p. 95.

87. "The Mythical Collapse of Historical Christianity," p. 744.

88. "The Jesus of History and the Christ of Religion," p. 209.

CHAPTER THREE
PAUL AND THE GOSPEL ABOUT JESUS

I: *The Life of Paul*:

Bacon accepted virtually all the epistles traditionally ascribed to Paul,[1] and in face of the "new chronology" advocated by H. J. Holtzmann, von Harnack and Sir William Ramsay, embraced the earlier, Eusebian chronology of the apostle's life.[2] Writing of Paul's conversion, Bacon stated that the apostle was at once unprepared and prepared for it.[3] He was unprepared insofar as he had not resided in Jerusalem during the period marked by the careers of Jesus and the Baptist.[4] On the other hand, he had set out on the Damascus road "something more than a Pharisee."[5] All the defenses of Paul's Pharisaic self-righteousness, honey-combed with misgivings, were on the point of crumbling,[6] and his mind was advancing toward an "unstable equilibrium."[7] Paul's knowledge of the glorified Jesus was thus an undeniable, though unconscious factor in his conversion.[8] Summarizing Paul's contradictory state of mind, Bacon wrote that the data of the apostle's "mystical experience" were all present to his consciousness, however unwelcome.[9]

From his "appreciation of differences" in Acts 9-13 and Galatians 1, Bacon concluded that Luke had diminished Paul's role in the Gentile mission. As a result, the apostle's career in the interval between his work in Syria-Cilicia and his return to Jerusalem (cf. Galatians 2:1) appeared to be a labor for Jews alone.[10] Here, said Bacon, it was better to reject the representation of Acts than to "bring the oath of Galatians 1:20 so near the brink of perjury."[11] This application of an "appreciation of differences" suggested to Bacon that Paul himself had authored Gentile, Hellenistic

Christianity which was subsequently developed by his greatest pupil and successor at Ephesus — the Fourth Evangelist. Yet, as late as 1915, Bacon continued to contest the hypothesis of an Ephesian imprisonment. Only toward the end of his career did he capitulate before mounting pressure and suggest that the reference to Andronicus in Romans 16 (a chapter which Bacon argued was intended for Ephesus)[12] as a "fellow prisoner" supplied the missing link between an Ephesian sojourn and imprisonment.[13] Once the Romans passage appeared to vindicate the theory of an Ephesian imprisonment, Bacon revised his earlier hypothesis. The doxology in Romans now suggested a pre-Pauline Christianity whose proportions were vaster than he had earlier supposed.[14]

Armed with these "dreams and imaginings" without which he believed historical research lacked "creative power,"[15] Bacon attempted the following reconstruction of the pre-Pauline Gentile mission:

When the little company of Jesus' five hundred disciples came down from Galilee to Jerusalem, its number was expanded to thousands recruited from the Baptist's followers who had been closely affiliated with the pre-Christian sect of the Essenes, and for whom John's baptism was already a sacrament of initiation.[16] The nascent church thus gave every indication of being an adaptation of current forms of sectarian practice, both Baptist and Essene.[17] Luke, however, condensed this extended process of coalescence in Acts 1 and 2; merged the Galileans under Peter and James with the Judean Baptists, and assigned to Peter (e.g., in Acts 2:38) responsibility for adopting the Baptist sacrament in Christian form.[18] Thus, Bacon continued, resulted that inconsistency in Luke's narrative, according to which the Gentiles were evangelized by those who had been scattered abroad after Stephen's death and knew no other baptism than John's.[19] Accordingly, the true founders of Christian mission were Hellenist refugees,[20] or that Greek-speaking branch of the Church under Stephen[21] and Philip which had fled Jerusalem after Stephen's death.[22]

For Bacon, the essential question concerning Paul's career, and especially that of his independence from the Jerusalem caliphate, emerged from out of a discrepancy between Luke's account of the apostolic council in Acts 15 and Paul's own utterances in Galatians 2. Bacon thoroughly agreed with Baur that Luke had minimized the conflict between Paul and the Jerusalem apostles concerning the law. But he could not, as already noted,[23] agree with Baur's contention that the original contestants were never reconciled. By way of an "appreciation of differences," Bacon proceeded to reconstruct what Luke had veiled and thus to modify Baur's scheme. He stated the problem thusly:

Galatians 2 knows nothing of an apostolic council called to settle the question of Jewish and Gentile table fellowship and charging Paul with the dissemination of its decrees.[24] Paul, recalling his Jerusalem visit in Galatians 2, refers only to a "private" conference with "the pillars."[25] Hence, the exception to his disallowing influence from the side of the "pillars" — "only they would have us remember the poor" (Galatians 2:10) — excludes such specific stipulations as appear in Acts 15:29.[26] On the other hand, the council and decrees of Acts 15:13-15 are historical,[27] supplementing Galatians 2:12 at a strategic point by describing the conclave issuing in the disturbance noted in the latter passage. Such decrees, Bacon contended, were actually enacted.[28] The problem arose, he continued, from the fusion of the conclave referred to in Acts 15:19-35 with that noted in Galatians 2:10 and which Bacon identified with Acts 11:30 and 12:25.[29] Since, wrote Bacon, the two questions of the Gentiles' relation to the law and the behavior of Jews among Gentiles were not settled simultaneously, introduction of the question of Gentile obligation to the law in Acts 15 is misplaced and premature.[30] The Western revisers of Acts 15 merely compounded the confusion by moralizing the "decrees" in 15:23-29.[31] Bacon concluded that the result of the fusion was to portray Paul as distributing the decrees throughout his churches and thus appropriating a point of view held by his enemies.[32]

Having stated the problem, Bacon attempted the following reconstruction:

After fourteen years of unmolested work among the Gentiles, Paul encountered opposition from Judea. Fearing his work might be jeopardized, he went to Jerusalem to lay his Gospel before the "pillars." From this conference was born the principle of mutual non-interference (Galatians 2:1-10; Acts 15:1-12), and a resulting division of mission fields.[33] The Gentiles were acknowledged to be free from obligation to Mosaic law, but the question concerning Jews who wished to keep the law but not without withdrawing from fellowship with Gentiles was left unanswered.[34] Paul quitted the conference convinced that everything needful for his mission had been conceded, and Peter, now having arrived at Antioch, followed his example.[35] At this point, however, an unforeseen contingency arose — "false brethren,"[36] i.e., a delegation from James,[37] could not leave unchallenged a construction which would release Jews from obligation to the law.[38] Equipped with the decrees of Acts 15:23-29 which prescribed for mixed communities[39] and which spuriously applied the principle of mutual non-interference to the question of table fellowship,[40] this delegation persuaded Peter and the rest that they were not at liberty to disregard the law.[41] Returning from Galatia, Paul and Barnabas found the church at Antioch divided.[42] In the bitter struggle which ensued, Paul and his churches appealed to their conference with the "pillars," not to the council and its decrees.[43]

From a comparison of Acts with the remainder of the Pauline corpus, Bacon contended that the resolution of the conflict had begun in Paul's lifetime and undertook this further revision of Baur's scheme:

The attempt of Peter's followers to achieve a *modus vivendi* found Paul prepared to go more than halfway.[44] Indeed, Paul's "olive branch" was the Jerusalem collection. The apostle had thus not been false to that first agreement with the "pillars" when they asked that he only "remember the poor," but personally effected, or at least witnessed the great reconciliation for which he is seen risking his life in Romans 15:30-33.[45]

II. *The Pauline Theology*:

Bacon saw Paul's theology oriented about a "teaching of the cup" and a "teaching about baptisms," an orientation he believed was also reflected in the arrangement of the synoptic materials. The "teaching of the cup" or "doctrine of the justifying blood,"[46] epitomized in I Corinthians 15:1,[47] announced justification by faith for Jew and Gentile.[48] Bacon fixed the origin of this teaching, symbolized in the Lord's Supper, in the pre-Pauline doctrine of baptism as a token of personal adherence to Jesus.[49] The "teaching of baptisms" or "life in the Spirit,"[50] symbolized in the baptismal rite and epitomized in I Corinthians 10:1-4,[51] Bacon described as an inseparable complement to the "teaching of the cup."

Bacon asserted that Paul was "almost" incredibly disregardful of the sayings and doings of Jesus,[52] though he maintained the chasm between contemporary faith and "primitive Nazarene Messianism" could only be bridged by an understanding of Paul.[53] For Bacon, the "greater epistles of Paul" — Romans, I and II Corinthians and Galatians, together with those portions of Acts 16-18 known as the "We" or "Travel Document" — reflected the actual personal character of Jesus.[54] Accordingly, the elements of Paul's Gospel as signaled in the two foci had their foundation in authentic sayings of Jesus.[55] Bacon continued that both the ethical and practical aspects of Paul's Gospel took their root from the life and teaching of the historical Jesus.[56] He naturally admitted that the Pauline letters only indirectly revealed the situation of belief and practice in Jesus' time. Such indirectness, however, was necessary, since the true basis of faith lay in the combination of what older witnesses had seen with the "eye of the flesh" with the values of what Paul had seen with the "eye of the spirit."[57] To the question, what would remain if all those elements belonging to interpretation were subtracted from the record and nothing remained but what could be inferred from Paul's incidental references, Bacon replied:

> Still we should have enough. We should know of one Leader in the
> history of man's quest for the life of God, whose ideal was all that
> the loftiest aspiration can conceive.[58]

He then added, "thank God that there is much more than
this."[59] But, to the extent Bacon regarded the basis of faith as
lying both in the tradition of Jesus' sayings and doings as
well as in the "truly apostolic and critically unimpeachable
gospel of Paul,"[60] to that extent he insisted that the success of
a liberal theology depended upon a return to Paul.[61]

Bacon first of all distinguished the gospel which Paul
"received" from that which he "proclaimed." The former he
described as the "resurrection Gospel" or "Gospel of
Jesus."[62] Peter, Bacon contended, not Paul, was the founder
of this resurrection faith,[63] and since Peter's "inner"
experience after Golgotha became the pattern in all respects
for Paul's,[64] it is possible to gain a reasonably accurate idea
of Peter's experience from Paul's own testimony.[65] Bacon
further described Paul's concept of Jesus' earthly work and
ministry as essentially "Galilean" or Petrine, rooted in the
Isaian ideal of the Suffering Servant.[66] At the same time, he
noted in Paul's doctrine of the atonement a non-Petrine but
nevertheless typically Jewish supplement to the Isaian
portrait. For Paul, the Servant was not merely anointed to
proclaim good tidings, but suffered for the sins of the world
and thus effected a cosmic redemption — an idea with its
roots in the history of Jewish martyrology and apocalyptic.[67]
Bacon noted that Paul avoided the "cruder" form of the
doctrine of substitution according to which Jesus died "in
our stead" rather than "for us" or "for our advantage."[68]
With this exception noted, he concluded that inasmuch as
the Servant doctrine comprised the primitive, original,
Petrine Gospel,[69] in its basic origin Paul's Christology was
identical with Peter's.[70]

Bacon then described the Gospel Paul proclaimed as the
pre-creative Wisdom of God.[71] That is, for Paul, Jesus had
become a "mediating hypostasis,"[72] the incarnation of the
redemptive spirit of the divine love.[73] The result, Bacon
wrote, was a Son of God Christology in contrast to the

nationalistic Son of David ideal.[74] Though Bacon regarded
this Wisdom-doctrine as rooted in the authentic teaching of
Jesus himself,[75] he nonetheless described the adjustment of
the Petrine Servant to Wisdom as distinctively new and
ultimately assigned it to the pre-Pauline, Hellenistic
community on Gnostic soil.[76] All this in contrast to the
Tübingen school which had posited almost a century for the
development of the Logos doctrine.[77] Thus, wrote Bacon,
the real point of transition as reflected in Paul's Christology
was the adoption of the Hellenistic, Hochmah writers'
hypostasis of the divine Wisdom.[78] To admit this, he said,
was to concede that mythology had entered the Gospel
story.[79] On the other hand, Bacon defended Paul from the
charge of syncretism by stating that the apostle did not
associate the incarnate Wisdom or Logos with a
metaphysical principle.[80] Indeed, Paul's use of the poetic
imagery of Hellenism was justified by the fact that it was not
possible for him to preach on Hellenistic soil without
employing such phraseology and ideas.[81]

Bacon continued that the companion to this idea of
Christ as Servant-Wisdom was Paul's notion of union with
Christ.[82] He interpreted Paul as preaching that the
precreative choice of the Son involved as his complement a
redeemed people.[83] From this standpoint the doctrine of
Jesus' supernatural birth could be applied to Christians
generally,[84] a concept entirely compatible with Judaism.[85] In
critical reference to Josiah Royce's concept of the "beloved
community," however, Bacon wrote that Paul could never
be construed as assenting to a formula wherein the mystical
body is everything and the head vanishes. He stated that
precisely because the Christ of Paul is no longer "a mere
individual human being" the apostle could proclaim
salvation in his name.[86] Bacon was aware that to the
historian of religions Paul's concept of union with Christ
might not appear novel but merely an appropriation of the
ancient Stoic figure of humanity as one vast, coherent and
living whole.[87] Yet, he distanced Paul from Stoicism and the
mysteries by stating that in contrast to the former Paul
declared that the Spirit which animates the Body and alone

can give it unity of life must be the Spirit of Christ.[88] In contrast to the latter, Paul had conceived the vision in the Christian's experience as a means of moral transformation.[89]

According to Bacon, this concept of union was not without effect on Paul's eschatology. It actually spelled the displacement of the apostle's earlier, more "primitive" view. Bacon wrote that in I and II Thessalonians, Paul had anticipated two great apocalyptic events. The first was that of the "mystery of iniquity," a concept originating in the Danielic prophecy of a temple profanation and evoked by Caligula's attempt to raise an altar to Zeus in the Jerusalem temple.[90] Since, however, Caligula's death made it impossible for the "abomination of desolation" to assume the material form awaited in the crisis of A.D. 40, Paul substituted a person for the object.[91] According to Bacon, the second event anticipated by Paul was the visible manifestation of Jesus as Son of Man.[92] In the later epistles, however, this concept began to retreat before the idea of the "Heavenly Man."[93] This appropriation of the concept of the "Heavenly Man" and its corollary, union with Christ, resulted in Paul's adaptation of the idea of the "abomination," and in his revision of the entire primitive eschatology.[94]

Bacon went on to comment that what was at once novel and temporary in Paul's theology was his concept of law. What was in a peculiar sense Paul's own and for which he was not dependent upon predecessors, was the doctrine that the cross at one stroke abolished the servile relation to God implied in the legalistic scheme.[95] Paul's stance toward the law thus implied a change in the cosmic economy of God, a substitution of the filial for the legal relationship. Speaking to the "temporary" aspect of Paul's doctrine, Bacon stated that it might never have been developed had not Paul been forced to defend the simple gospel of salvation against detractors who declared that he had "made the law of none effect."[96] This very necessity for defense, Bacon concluded, rendered this particular feature in Paul's theology contingent and of only temporary value.[97]

Bacon, writing that Ephesus and the churches of Asia observed the Passion on Nisan 14th rather than on the 15th, stated that Paul sanctioned and approved such celebration.[98] He drew support for this contention from what he believed to be reflections of ritual in I Corinthians 15:3f., particularly in vs. 20, which compares the risen Christ to the "wave sheaf" of new corn lifted up before God in the ritual of "first fruits."[99] Therefore, the day on which Christ became "the first fruits of those who have fallen asleep" was that on which the lambs were slaughtered in preparation for Passover. According to Jewish reckoning, then, Nisan 16, as it had been in the year A.D. 33 or 34, was "the third day" after the crucifixion.[100]

Summarizing Paul's theology, Bacon wrote that for the apostle as for Jesus, the visible agency of the living, redeeming God lay at the basis of all his thought. But, he insisted, Paul would never have learned to think in such fashion without Jesus — he would have remained a Pharisee to the end. Through the agency of the historical Jesus, then, Paul came to a knowledge of the living God.[101] To the objection that the Pauline doctrine of the incarnate One had little support in Jesus' actual teaching, Bacon replied that we need not proceed beyond the simple fact that Jesus himself had a doctrine of the present, redeeming Spirit of God,[102] and summed up Paul's relation to Jesus and to the faith of the earliest community in two paragraphs, one written toward the beginning, the other toward the end of his career:

> It is just this personality of Paul which explains the transition of Christianity from a spiritualized type of Jewish messianism to a world-religion, satisfactory both to the instincts of individual religion . . . and at the same time to the speculative logic of philosophy. . . . [103]

> God needed a theologian to teach men that the gospel is the thing that He does and will do through the agency of this eternal Christ of mankind. . . . God needed an ambassador of peace to the world.[104]

1. *An Introduction to the New Testament*, pp. 128, 277. On the other hand, cf. pp. 140ff.; *The Making of the New Testament*, pp. 84f., 89.

2. "A Criticism of the New Chronology of Paul (Concluded)," *The Expositor*, X (1899), p. 430.

3. *The Story of St. Paul*, p. 37.

4. "The Gospel Paul 'Received,'" *The American Journal of Theology*, XXI (1917), p. 25; cf. *Jesus The Son Of God or Primitive Christology*, Three Essays and a Discussion (New Haven: Yale University Press, 1911), p. 99.

5. *The Story of St. Paul*, p. 23.

6. *Ibid.*, p. 38.

7. "The Mystical Experience of St. Paul," *At One With the Invisible*, ed. E. Hershey Sneath (New York: The Macmillan Co., 1921), p. 112.

8. *The Story of St. Paul*, p. 58.

9. "The Mystical Experience of St. Paul," p. 111.

10. *The Story of St. Paul*, pp. 82, 85; "The Gospel Paul 'Received'," p. 26; "Professor Harnack on the Lukan Narrative," *The American Journal of Theology*, XIII (1909), p. 67; "Acts versus Galatians," pp. 461ff.; "The Chronological Scheme of Acts," *The Harvard Theological Review*, XIV (1921), p. 156f.; "Some 'Western' Variants in the Text of Acts," p. 123f.; "Stephen's Speech: Its Argument and Doctrinal Relationship," *Historical and Critical Contributions to Biblical Science*, Yale Bicentennial Volume (New York: Scribners, 1902), p. 216; *The Making of the New Testament*, p. 57.

11. "Acts versus Galatians," p. 456.

12. "The Doxology at the End of Romans," *Journal of Biblical Literature*, XVIII (1899), p. 172; "Andronicus," pp. 300ff.

13. "Andronicus," pp. 300ff.

14. *Ibid.*, p. 304.

15. *Ibid.*

16. *The Gospel of the Hellenists* (New York: Henry Holt and Co., 1933), pp. 70, 88f.; "Is Baptism Syncretistic?" *Anglican Theological Review*, XIII (1931), p. 173f.

17. *The Gospel of the Hellenists*, cf. pp. 67 and 69.

18. "Is Baptism Syncretistic?" p. 174.

19. *Ibid.*

20. *The Gospel of the Hellenists*, p. 80.

21. *Jesus The Son of God*, p. 17.

22. *The Gospel of the Hellenists*, p. 80. The private files of Frank Porter contain shorthand notes and jottings on Bacon's studies. In one note, Porter suggests that his own volume on Paul, which implied a more or less developed Greek Christology and thus a Hellenistic community independent of Paul, contributed to the modification of Bacon's earlier view. In another note, he writes that if indeed his Pauline

studies had influenced Bacon, the influence was reflected only in Bacon's posthumously published *The Gospel of the Hellenists*.

23. Cf. p. 12 above.
24. "Acts versus Galatians," p. 457.
25. *The Making of the New Testament*, p. 60.
26. *Commentary on The Epistle of Paul to the Galatians*, p. 62.
27. "Acts versus Galatians," p. 469.
28. *Commentary on The Epistle of Paul to the Galatians*, p. 125; "Professor Harnack on the Lukan Narrative," p. 74.
29. *Commentary on The Epistle of Paul to the Galatians*, p. 38.
30. "Acts versus Galatians," pp. 470, 473; *An Introduction to the New Testament*, pp. 64, 67.
31. "Some 'Western' Variants in the Text of Acts," p. 134f.
32. *Commentary on The Epistle of Paul to the Galatians*, p. 125; "Professor Harnack on the Lukan Narrative," pp. 74, 76; "A Century of Change in New Testament Criticism," p. 616.
33. "The Apostolic Decree against ΠΟΡΝΕΙΑ," *The Expositor*, VII (1914), p. 41; *An Introduction to the New Testament*, p. 64; *Commentary on The Epistle of Paul to the Galatians*, p. 125.
34. *Commentary on The Epistle of Paul to the Galatians*, p. 119.
35. "Peter's Triumph at Antioch," *The Journal of Religion*, IX (1929), p. 214f.
36. *An Introduction to the New Testament*, p. 66.
37. "A Century of Change in New Testament Criticism," p. 616; "Acts versus Galatians," p. 469.
38. *An Introduction to the New Testament*, p. 66.
39. *Ibid.*, p. 66f.
40. *Commentary on The Epistle of Paul to the Galatians*, p. 125.
41. "A Century of Change in New Testament Criticism," p. 616. Bacon declared that Otto Pfleiderer's description of Peter's conduct as arising from misgivings over Gentile laxity was "behind the times," and insisted that Peter's vascillation rooted in compunctions concerning his own laxity; cf. "Primitive Christianity," p. 758f.
42. "Peter's Triumph at Antioch," p. 215.
43. *The Making of the New Testament*, pp. 60, 67.
44. *Ibid.*, p. 68.
45. *An Introduction to the New Testament*, p. 14.
46. "Reflections of Ritual in Paul," *The Harvard Theological Review*, VIII (1915), p. 524.
47. *Ibid.*
48. "John as Preacher of Justification by Faith," *The Expositor*, XVI (1918), p. 193.
49. *The Gospel of the Hellenists*, pp. 340-42.
50. *The Apostolic Message: A Historical Inquiry* (New York: The Century Co., 1925), p. 396.
51. "Reflections of Ritual in Paul." p. 524.

52. "Recent Aspects of the Johannine Problem: III. Indirect Internal Evidence," *The Hibbert Journal*, III (1905), p. 359.
53. *The Story of St. Paul*, p. 4f.; "Jesus Christ," p. 161.
54. "The Success and Failure of Liberalism," p. 97; *The Story of Jesus and the Beginnings of the Church*, p. 5; "The Mythical Collapse of Historical Christianity," p. 736.
55. "The 'Other' Comforter," *The Expositor*, XIV (1917), p. 281; cf. "The Sacrament of Footwashing," *The Expository Times*, XLIII (1931), p. 220f.
56. "Jesus Christ," p. 162; *Christianity Old and New*, p. 127.
57. *Jesus and Paul*, p. 167.
58. *Ibid.*, p. 168; cf. "The Teaching Ministry for To-Morrow," p. 14.
59. *Jesus and Paul*, p. 169.
60. "The Success and Failure of Liberalism," p. 97.
61. *Ibid.*, p. 104.
62. *Christianity Old and New*, p. 70f.
63. *Ibid.*, p. 100; *Jesus The Son Of God or Primitive Christology*, p. 98.
64. *The Apostolic Message*, p. 396.
65. *Ibid.*, p. 148.
66. "The Gospel Paul 'Received'," p. 33; *The Apostolic Message*, p. 368.
67. *The Apostolic Message*, p. 368; cf. *Commentary on The Epistle of Paul to the Galatians*, p. 110.
68. *Commentary on The Epistle of Paul to the Galatians*, p. 48.
69. *The Apostolic Message*, pp. 186f., 398.
70. *Jesus The Son Of God or Primitive Christology*, p. 87; cf. *The Story of Jesus and the Beginnings of the Church*, p. 287, and *Jesus and Paul*, p. 59.
71. "Alpha and Omega," *A Dictionary of Christ and the Gospels*, ed. James Hastings (New York: Charles Scribner's Sons, 1906), I, 45; *The Apostolic Message*, p. 167.
72. "Alpha and Omega," p. 44.
73. *The Apostolic Message*, p. 166; *Jesus The Son of God*, p. 18.
74. *The Story of Jesus and the Beginnings of the Church*, p. 74.
75. "Wisdom," *A Dictionary of Christ and the Gospels*, II, 829.
76. *The Gospel of the Hellenists*, pp. 80, 86, 88f., 94, 100, 110.
77. *Is Mark a Roman Gospel?* p. 4f.
78. "Immortality in the Fourth Gospel," p. 285; "The Relations of New Testament Science to Kindred Sciences," p. 580; *The Story of St. Paul*, pp. 326, 329.
79. "The Mythical Collapse of Historical Christianity," p. 743.
80. "Immortality in the Fourth Gospel," p. 285; "'The Resurrection' in Byzantine Art," *The Interpreter*, XVII (1920), p. 29f.; "The Mythical Collapse of Historical Christianity," p. 743; cf. "The Relations of New Testament Science to Kindred Sciences," p. 575.
81. *The Story of St. Paul*, p. 310.
82. Cf. "St. Paul's Message to Religion," *The Constructive Quarterly*, I (1913), p. 181, and "The Return to Theology," p. 123.

83. *An Introduction to the New Testament*, p. 111f.; "Supplementary Note on the Aorist εὐδόκησα, Mark 1:1, *Journal of Biblical Literature*, XX (1901), p. 29.

84. *Commentary on The Epistle of Paul to the Galatians*, p. 93.

85. *Is Mark a Roman Gospel?* p. 89.

86. "Royce's Interpretation of Christianity," *The Philosophical Review*, XXV (1916), pp. 327ff.

87. "The Epistle of Moral Preparedness. Its Contribution to the Present Situation," *The Congregationalist*, CII (1917), p. 479.

88. *Ibid.*

89. "The Mystical Experience of St. Paul," p. 129; *The Story of St. Paul*, pp. 77, 80; *The Making of the New Testament*, p. 96.

90. "Wrath 'Unto the Uttermost,'"*The Expositor*, XXIV (1922), pp. 364f., 369; *The Gospel of Mark, Its Composition and Date* (New Haven: Yale University Press, 1925), pp. 96-98; *An Introduction to the New Testament*, p. 77.

91. *The Gospel of Mark, Its Composition and Date*, pp. 96, 98; "La date et l'origine de l'Evangile selon Marc," *Revue d'Histoire et de Philosophie Religieuses*, III (1923), p. 276; "Imperialism and the Christian Ideal," *Yale Review*, IV (1915), p. 467.

92. "Wrath 'Unto the Uttermost,'" p. 365.

93. Cf. "The Festival of Lives Given for the Nation in Jewish and Christian Faith," *The Hibbert Journal*, XV (1917), p. 273.

94. *The Story of St. Paul*, p. 76, n. 1.

95. "The Gospel Paul 'Received'," p. 27.

96. *The Making of the New Testament*, p. 14; *Jesus and Paul*, p. 97.

97. "St. Paul's Message to Religion," p. 181.

98. "The Resurrection in Primitive Tradition and Observance," p. 391.

99. "Reflections of Ritual in Paul," pp. 506, 508.

100. "Raised The Third Day," *The Expositor*, XXVI (1923), p. 440.

101. *He Opened To Us The Scriptures*, p. 91.

102. "St. Paul's Message to Religion," p. 181f.

103. "Primitive Christianity," p. 761.

104. "The Return to Theology," p. 119.

CHAPTER FOUR
THE GOSPEL OF JESUS

I: *The Earliest Witnesses:*

Bacon contended that the church knew only two types of Gospel composition — "sayings and doings," corresponding to the "gospel of" and "about Jesus." These types, he wrote, furnish the clue to the two foci about which the anecdotes in the synoptic Gospels were agglutinated — Baptism and the Supper[1] — and, as earlier noted,[2] provided the orientation for Paul's teaching. Since, said Bacon, Jesus' career had begun with the one and ended with the other, the arrangement was dictated simply and purely by historical fact.[3] Thus, for example, Mark is agglomerative in structure, giving it a "that reminds me" style.[4] This lack of chronological interest, Bacon continued, not Mark's style, Papias referred to when he spoke of the evangelist's lack of order.[5] Bacon then described the first half of Mark's Gospel as developing the baptismal theme, symbol of the doctrine of life in the Spirit, and the second as concentrating on the theme of the eucharistic cup, symbol of the doctrine of justification.[6]

A. The "P" Narrative:

With an eye to the ancient tradition, Bacon asserted that there are scenes in Mark's Gospel which have Peter's narrative for their origin.[7] Though he rejected the theory of a written Proto-Mark,[8] he did assume the existence of an "original Roman form" of the Gospel[9] not used by Matthew and Luke.[10] The backbone of this "Ur-Marcus" Bacon termed the "P" narrative,[11] reflecting Galilean, Palestinian tradition, composed in Aramaic, and based on or modified

by the memorabilia of Peter.[12] Bacon believed that traces of
belief in Jesus' Davidic descent were due to this document as
well as reflections of the Isaian Servant overlaid by a Son of
Man doctrine appropriated by the final redactor from Q and
adapted to the Pauline Son of God.[13] Mark's distinction
between the baptism of John and that of Jesus as a baptism
of the Spirit may also have been due to the influence of the
"P" narrative. A certain deference toward Peter reflected the
same influence.[14] Bacon saw further evidence of the Petrine
source in Mark's portrayal of Jesus as assuming the role of
the expected Deliverer of Israel.[15] Finally, Bacon believed
reflections of this "Galilean strain" or "P" narrative could be
seen in Mark 10, counterpart of Matthew's Sermon on the
Mount, as well as in the evangelist's fundamentally Jewish
world-view. This original "Roman form" or "Proto-Mark,"
Bacon concluded, finally disappeared, due to conflict with
its more acceptable rival during the controversy with the
Docetists over the question of authentic Petrine tradition.[16]

B. The Second Synoptic Source:

Asserting that our present Gospel of Mark yielded a
primary source for the Gospels of Matthew and Luke, Bacon
believed he found traces of still another source in "Redactor
Mark's" and his co-evangelists' dependence upon the
literature of Lyric Wisdom.[17] For Bacon, such passages as
Mark 4:11; Matthew 11:25-30 and Luke 10:21-22, together
with the agraphon in I Corinthians 1:18-3:1 and the
Johannine Logos doctrine, all rooted in the Wisdom
literature.[18] From the similarity in their use of this material,
Bacon concluded that all four Gospel writers supplemented
the fundamental Petrine narrative with material from a
document "S."[19] This document, Bacon wrote, was to be
distinguished from the double-tradition material in
Matthew and Luke commonly called "Q," and which merely
reflected that earlier, written "Second Source."[20]

"S," wrote Bacon, was once current in Aramaic,[21] and in
this form was used and translated by Redactor Mark.[22]
When used by Matthew and Luke, however, it was in
Greek.[23] Bacon agreed that the sources of the sources of the

later synoptic Gospels may indeed have been in Aramaic,
and was even willing to concede that none of Luke's written
sources were Greek.[24] He argued, however, that such a fact
actually destroyed the argument of his university colleague
C. C. Torrey for the early date or apostolic origin of a Gospel
based upon the translation-Greek of its sources, since the
absence of any Semitic flavor might have excluded the
writing altogether.[25] In general, Bacon insisted that

> no amount of Semitic coloration . . . can set aside the long
> established and scientifically demonstrated fact that the two
> common sources on the basis of which the later Synoptic Gospels
> are principally made up are the Greek documents Mark and S.[26]

Bacon assigned document "S" to Syrian Antioch,[27]
contending that it neither enjoyed nor claimed apostolic
prestige[28] and was not to be connected with "Matthew."[29] He
further asserted that the "Second Source" was a true *diegesis*
or narrative.[30] "S" thus gave an account of Jesus' ministry in
Galilee and reported how it was received by the common
people but rejected by the synagogue.[31]

Bacon distinguished two forms of this "Second
Source," the one comprising an original narrative of simpler,
"Caesarean" form, developed in the direction of "gnomic
expansion"[32] — in this form known to Matthew and
Luke — and the other, a later, "Jerusalem" form, developed
in the direction of "biographic expansion"[33] and known only
to Luke.[34] Thus Matthew's alteration of the original order of
"S" may not have been due to his own revising, but to the
exemplar of "S" available to him.[35] At the same time, wrote
Bacon, the reason for Matthew's and Luke's failure to
preserve any considerable trace of the outline of "S" lay in
their "exaggerated respect" for Mark.[36]

As to the content of "S," Bacon stated that the Baptist
played a major role, which began to be deemphasized in
Mark, due to the desire to identify the Baptist with Elijah
redivivus.[37] Further, this "Second Source" set Jesus forth as
the Wisdom of God, the Isaian Servant, vainly pleading with
a wayward people and bringing the Gentiles to justification

by revealing his Father.[38] For this reason, said Bacon, such key terms in "S" as "repentance," "faith" and "justification" require interpretation in light of their connection with Isaiah and Lyric Wisdom.[39] Concluding that "S" had a definite anti-legalistic bent,[40] Bacon wrote that its characteristics were the very same which dominate in Peter and Paul.[41] "S" was therefore one of the first written attempts at combining the "gospel of" with the "gospel about Jesus," the "doings" with the "sayings."[42] To this "Gospel of the Teachings," Bacon assigned an importance rivaled only by the "We" sections in Acts.[43]

C. The "Q" Source:

To their use of Mark and "S," Bacon added Matthew's and Luke's use of "Q," a designation which he reserved exclusively for the Matthaean and Lukan "double-tradition" material drawn from document "S," and not available to Mark.[44] "Q" was thus not coextensive with "S," nor to be identified with the compilation of "Logia" attributed to Matthew by Papias.[45] Because of its relationship to "S," however, "Q's" material stood closer than Mark to historical fact.[46]

Bacon regarded "Q" as an agglutination of sayings into discourses in which narrative outline was subordinated to didactic aims.[47] Though he assigned to Luke considerable dislocation of the original order of "Q,"[48] due, no doubt, to Luke's own special source,[49] he still believed Luke gave to "Q" its most fully developed form and thus constituted a more trustworthy reproduction than the order and text of Matthew.[50]

With respect to the content of "Q," Bacon asserted that it did far more justice to John's greatness and the significance of the movement he instituted,[51] and therefore deserved priority over Mark.[52] As did "S," "Q" depicted the career of Jesus as meeting the clearly conceived Messianic ideal of the Isaian Servant.[53] Noting that the Jesus of "Q" rejects the exorcist's fame and seeks only the glory of his Father,[54] Bacon contended that at this point Matthew joins hands with Paul since such traits dominate in the Pauline conception.[55] Thus "Q," in contrast to the anti-legalism of "S," represented the Gospel as a royal law[56] — a feature which Bacon asserted was more authentic than Mark's and "S's" anti-legal portrayal.

D. Additional Sources:

To "S's" influence on Mark Bacon added the influence of other Pauline sources,[57] and in addition described Mark as dependent on materials from Matthew and Luke.[58] This dependence, however, was not to be construed in terms of Mark's dependence on canonical Matthew and Luke, but rather upon a Greek translation of "S" together with other materials used by the two Synoptists.[59]

In addition to Markan-Petrine tradition, Bacon assigned to Matthew a special Aramaic source "N" or "Nazarene Targum," a collection of "fungoid developments on the stock of Markan tradition,"[60] corresponding in style and character to such pseudo-apostolic compositions as the Gospel of the Hebrews, the Ebionite Pseudo-Matthew, the Gospel of the Egyptians, the Gospel of Peter and an apocryphon appearing in Ignatius.[61] From this source, originating among Jewish-Christians of Palestine, Bacon derived the Matthaean genealogy and infancy chapters together with formula-quotations which still show traces of the Hebrew text and which Matthew's redactor did not alter except where special interest required a change.[62] He also assigned a portion of Matthew's account of the passion and resurrection to this source.[63] Once he had subtracted "M" (Markan-Petrine tradition) together with "S" and "N," Bacon concluded that the remaining materials derived from Christian or non-Christian oral tradition, from Luke's special source, and from Matthew's own redaction.[64]

Bacon added to Luke's use of Mark, "S" and "Q" a special source which he designated "L," or, following B. H. Streeter, "Proto-Luke."[65] Further, Bacon distinguished two editions of "L." The first constituted a primitive form, entirely independent of the final author or redactor.[66] The second he described as an edition of "L" which had undergone revision since the appearance of Mark's Gospel.[67] To this source, revised or unrevised, Bacon on occasion credited the use of "S," but not in a form identical with that known to Matthew. For this reason, he wrote, one need not posit an "M" source accessible only to Matthew in order to explain the discrepancies between Luke's and Matthew's use of "S" or "Q."[68] To these Lukan sources, Bacon then added the evangelist's use of oral Jewish material in his genealogy and infancy chapters,[69] originating in the latter part of the century among Jewish Christians of Palestine.[70] The remainder of Luke's Gospel Bacon assigned to the survival of oral tradition or to the redactor.[71]

Bacon regarded Luke's second volume as an attempt to wed two essentially conflicting sources. The one he described as Jerusalemite, Aramaic, the "canonical counterpart of 'S'," reminiscent of such apocryphal Gospels as the Acts of Peter, and for which the transfiguration story formed the pivot.[72] The other source Bacon defined as Antiochene, Greek, containing the Acts of Paul, but independent of the Pauline epistolary literature.[73] Bacon stated that the author of Acts had adjusted two conflicting sources in chapters 6-12 by way of transposition, with the result that Peter's evangelization of the Gentiles was made to precede Paul's.[74]

Thus, though Bacon embraced the thesis of C. C. Torrey regarding an Aramaic source beneath Acts 1-15 and distinguished it from still another Greek document used in the remainder of the book, he did not regard "First" and "Second Acts" as identical with the "Aramaic Acts of Peter" and the "Greek Acts of Paul" which he believed underlay them both.[75]

In addition to these special sources, Bacon assumed Redactor Luke's use of Good Friday material in connection with the Stephen episode.[76] Further, according to Bacon, beneath "Second Acts" lay the "Travel Document," a source which he occasionally associated with Epaphroditus, delegate of the Philippian church, and whose diary he believed furnished the basis for the story of Paul's last journeys.[77] Most often, however, Bacon assigned the "Travel Document" to the Luke of Colossians 4:14.[78] But it was the redactor, eager to weld such obviously Pauline pieces as the diary together with his Petrine materials, who finally adjusted the "Travel Document" to the revised edition of Acts.[79]

II: *"What the Eye Saw"*— *The Gospel of Mark*:

Bacon described Mark's Gospel in terms of "what the eye saw," since he believed it consisted essentially of Peter's missionary discourses arranged to supply an outline of Jesus' public activity.[80] Writing that Mark was composed under circumstances which made the testimony of eyewitnesses inaccessible, Bacon denied that the Gospel was not composed with care, but contended it was not what it might have been had an apostle written it, and assumed a final redactor for the completed work. Thus, while he described the Gospel as the story of Peter as "preached" by Mark, Bacon viewed the ascription of authorship as due to the Gospel's authority among the Pauline churches.[81]

Bacon wrote that the "Little Apocalypse" in chapter 13 remained the best source regarding the date of Mark's composition.[82] He described that chapter as applying the prophecy of Daniel 11 to the situation in A.D. 39-40, making literal fulfillment impossible.[83] The evangelist had thus modified his text with the result that the "desolating sacrilege" approximated the "man of sin" in II Thessalonians.[84] While allowing for the possibility that the entire Gospel was composed in A.D. 40, Bacon found other "tribulations" reflected in chapter 13, leading him to posit a later hand which adapted texts first appearing in A.D. 40 to the event of the temple ruin.[85] He thus assigned to the Gospel a final composition not earlier than A.D. 70-71.[86]

Bacon agreed that Rome was by all odds the most probable source of the Gospel, "Peter's immigrant spiritual 'son' providing his venerable father with a new home in the West."[87] Noting Papias' statement that Mark had translated Peter's discourses from Aramaic into Greek, Bacon wrote that since the Aramaic used was not of one at home in the language, Papias' words must be distinguished from those of his informant, the Elder John of Jerusalem, whose remark did not intend to describe Mark as Peter's "interpreter" in any narrow sense.[88]

Bacon maintained that Mark's Gospel not only reflected practices and problems of the Gentile church between A.D. 70-90, but was also written to confirm and fortify the church's beliefs, institutions and rituals.[89] By applying aetiological method to the Gospel, he concluded that it concretely demonstrated

> the use to which primitive Palestinian material could be put by a great Greek-speaking, Gentile church, thoroughly Pauline in all its anti-Jewish tendencies, a decade or so after both Peter and Paul were dead.[90]

Bacon drew this conclusion from his examination of Mark's Christology, attitude toward the law and the Galilean disciples, as well as from his observation of what he called the Gospel's "reflections of ritual."

According to Bacon, Mark superimposed upon the ancient Jesus-tradition the theme of the Gentile demi-god, with the result that all the attributes of the glorified Lord were trajected back into Jesus' earthly life.[91] At the same time, Bacon believed he saw Pauline influence in Mark's portrayal of Jesus' sonship in ethical rather than metaphysical terms.[92] Indeed, wrote Bacon, when interpretation has been subtracted from the bulk of the Gospel, what remains can be inferred from Paul's own incidental references.[93] Mark thus furnished a "gospel about," and was relatively indifferent to the "gospel of Jesus."[94] At the same time, Bacon referred to the "ultra-" or "quasi-Pauline" character of the Gospel which he assigned to the final redactor.[95] This radicalism lay in an exchange of the idea of forgiveness for a doctrine of vicarious substitution; in a view of miracles as signs of Jesus' power,[96] and in the rejection of the idea of the incarnation of Wisdom in the Servant of God.[97] Bacon thus characterized the Gospel's Christology as a-genealogical, anti-Jewish or "defiantly independent" of the tradition concerning Christ's Davidic descent.[98]

Consonant with his conviction that synoptic tradition and thus, presumably, Redactor Mark had progressively departed from the "common Gospel,"[99] Bacon regarded Mark's concept of law as reflecting an antinomianism which even Paul himself had restrained.[100] This antinomianism had its anti-Jewish cast in Jesus' defiance of the law;[101] in the doctrine of Israel's "hardening" in chapter 4; in a "Corinthian" intolerance toward Jewish distinctions as reflected in chapter 7; and in the condemnation of Israel's leaders for their rejection of the two supreme manifestations of God's mercy — John's baptism and Jesus' offer of forgiveness.[102]

Bacon believed that Redactor Mark gave aid and comfort to a specifically Gentile, ultra-Pauline view through his deprecation of the Galilean apostles and kindred of Jesus. For the Redactor, the manifestation of the risen Lord to Peter was no longer the foundation of faith. Rather, the portrait of Peter as rallier of the deserters was replaced in 14:27-31 with a promise of Jesus to fulfill this task himself.[103] Bacon saw this anti-Galilean strain most clearly reflected in what he believed to be the story of the "lost ending" of Mark. "Primitive Mark," Bacon wrote, contained a "Galilean-Petrine version" which continued the "former" treatise ending at 15:39.[104] This version reported Jesus' appearance in Galilee to Peter and the eleven,[105] but was so contradictory of Luke's narrative and so disparaging toward Peter and the apostles that it disappeared.[106] The entire narrative was thus recast. Features were added from "Q" together with material from Luke's special source which detached Peter from the resurrection narrative and connected the latter with the story of the empty tomb.[107] Once Luke and Matthew were circulated, only what could be reconciled with Luke-Acts was retained.[108] The more graphic "shrine story" thus gained the field.[109] The later addition of 16:9-20 further adapted the Petrine-Galilean version to Luke-Acts, a still greater revolt against the apostolic resurrection story as narrated in I Corinthians 15.[110]

Regarding the Gospel's intent to explain and support the ritual practices of the community from which it emerged,

Bacon marked the influence of the Church's baptism on Mark, chapter 1. Similarly, he described the narrative of Jesus' empowering by the Spirit as influenced by the community's concept of the believer's reception of the word of wisdom and power.[111] Bacon treated every point in the feeding accounts of chapters 6 and 8 as of value for those who presided at the Agape — the arrangement of the multitude, the hour of the day, the thanksgiving, the distribution and gathering of fragments were all designed to fix the authority for the Church's practice in Jesus' example.[112]

In examining the passion and resurrection narratives, Bacon tried to identify the specific community and mode of observance to which the Gospel conforms. Noting Redactor Mark's identification of the Last Supper with the Passover — thus fixing the crucifixion on the 15th of Nisan — Bacon concluded that the passion narrative conformed to the anti-Quartodecimanian practice of the Roman community which celebrated Jesus' passion weekly as well as annually.[113] According to Bacon, Mark's noting of the watches of the day corresponded to the divisions in the day of fasting observed by the Roman church.[114] In this fashion, the Passover and vigil in Gethsemane served as models for the church's annual and hebdomadal observance.[115] Bacon concluded that the reference to Jesus' resurrection "after three days" derived from Roman ritual practice as influenced by the ancient, pre-Christian observance of the vernal equinox.[116]

III. *"What the Ear Heard"* — *The Gospels of Matthew and Luke*:

Subsuming the Gospels of Matthew and Luke under the above rubric,[117] Bacon noted that the name "Matthew" did not appear in the tradition prior to Papias who believed the Gospel to be a translation of Aramaic *Logia* composed by the apostle.[118] In later life, Bacon insisted that the verdict of criticism opposed this ancient notion, that Papias' and his informant's reference to the *canonical* Matthew was obvious

and undeniable.[119] Contending that the author of Matthew
was not an apostle,[120] Bacon stated that the Gospel's
association with Matthew was due to a transference rooting
in a conjecture applied to Matthew 9:9 and the call of Levi in
Mark 2:14.[121]

According to Bacon's earlier notion, a collection or
syntagma of Aramaic *logia* composed by the apostle
underlay our present Matthew,[122] and the subsequent Greek
edition constituted one version of that collection.[123] Bacon's
original enthusiasm over an announcement of the discovery
of the "dominical oracles" referred to by Papias was soon
dampened by his realization that the fragments in question
could not be identified with the *logia* of Matthew.[124] He
consequently abandoned his hypothesis and attributed the
impetus given the search for the "Matthaean Logia" to the
"ghost of Schleiermacher's dead theory" of oral Gospels.[125]
In his unpublished manuscript on synoptic tradition, he
expressed "deep regret" that he had followed the lead of H. J.
Holtzmann, the last great representative of the Aramaic
logia-hypothesis.[126]

Chapter 24 of Matthew furnished Bacon his basis for
dating the Gospel. He contended that the eschatological
discourse had been detached from the temple ruin and
converted into a prediction of the end of the world.[127] In this
fashion, Matthew had restored to the Danielic prediction its
original sense[128] and rekindled hope in the Parousia to
follow the worst sufferings of the Church.[129] From this
Bacon concluded that when Matthew put pen to paper, the
Church, having sustained the crisis reflected in Mark 13,
returned to Jerusalem only to prepare to leave it a second
time.[130] The Gospel therefore dated from the period A.D. 90-
100.[131]

Bacon fixed the Gospel's ˙origin in northern or
northeastern Syria.[132] From there, he stated, the Gospel was
carried to Antioch, and thence to Rome. Bacon first
suggested that Rome gave the Gospel the final seal of
approval following a visit from Ignatius,[133] but later
abandoned this suggestion and attributed the status
accorded Matthew from A.D. 120 onward to a Roman synod

called to determine whether the "new doctrines" of the star and Virgin Birth could be received.[134]

By uncovering Matthew's "method of pragmatic values," Bacon concluded that the Gospel demonstrates the use to which primitive materials could be put by a Syrian, Jewish-Christian, anti-Pauline, neo-legalistic community, and, as in Mark's case, drew his conclusions from the Gospel's Christology, attitude toward the law and the Galilean disciples, and from his observation of the Gospel's reflections of ritual.

To Bacon's mind, the Gospel's distinctively Jewish-Christian bias is reflected in the purpose to which Matthew put his birth and infancy narratives. He described the Gospel as clinging to the "older," Palestinian tradition of Jesus' human parentage, represented in the pedigree of 1:1-6, and saw its transformation of Jesus' sonship into a "prenatal adoption" as "toning down" the Markan, ultra-Pauline, adoptionist Christology which identified Jesus' sonship with his baptism.[135] The result, wrote Bacon, lay in Matthew's furnishing a bridge between the Palestinian doctrine of Jesus' human parentage and the *agenealogetos* Christology of Mark.[136] He further characterized the Gospel as revising Mark's "Little Apocalypse," by which Matthew attempted to foster the pre-exilic notion of Jesus as Danielic Son of Man, suppliant on Israel's behalf for the everlasting kingdom. Matthew had thus trajected into Jesus' mouth the apocalyptic use of the title "Son of Man" who distributes rewards and punishments in the end-time.[137] Bacon also saw an anti-Markan, anti-Pauline prejudice in Matthew's rejection of the theory of the demonic recognition of the Christ, and in his application of the Servant's bearing of sins to the healing of physical infirmities — evidence, added Bacon, of Matthew's sensitivity to the moral dangers of vicarious atonement in Mark's soteriology.[138] Bacon concluded that since Matthew represents the adjustment of the apostolic "gospel of the teaching" to the Pauline "gospel of the personality" and thus a swing of the pendulum away from Paul toward a Jewish "gospel of Jesus," northern or northeastern Syria, and Antioch in particular, was the center best represented by the Gospel's Christology.[139]

Bacon wrote that the Matthaean portrait of Jesus as Teacher of the Law or second Moses reflects a neo-legalistic, Syrian locale.[140] He believed this portrait corresponded with the Gospel's construction according to five books of Christian Torah or "Pereks," a term from Sir John Hawkins.[141] He stated that "Perek I," focusing in chapters 5-7, contains Jesus' sermon on "filial righteousness," and that "Perek II," focusing in chapter 10, treats of the "Mission of the Twelve" — its intent to provide the missionary with equipment and incentive for his work.[142] He entitled "Perek III," focusing in chapter 13 and influenced by the "exile section" in Mark 3:20-4:34, "The Formation of the Spiritual Israel."[143] "Perek IV," focusing in chapter 18, he described as enunciating the "Rule of the Brotherhood," and "Perek V," focusing in chapters 23-25, as dealing with the coming of the Son of Man.[144] Bacon continued that to each of these five artificial collections is joined a section of narrative introducing a speech of Jesus, each subsequent narrative then coupled with the preceding discourse by a colophon — "and when Jesus finished these sayings" — after the style of the Pentateuchal codes.[145] Finally, he described the five books as prefaced by an introduction (chapters 1-2) and completed by a closing narrative, thus yielding a seven-fold division of the Gospel.[146]

Bacon regarded the term "neo-legalist" as most applicable to Matthew,[147] and drew for his support on the evangelist's concept of faith as "thankworthy goodness" which as "man's grace" conforms to the divine standard and thus guarantees his heavenly reward.[148] For this reason, Matthew eliminates Jesus' disclaimer of goodness in 19:16ff.[149] Bacon uncovered a similar neo-legalism in the "Doom Chapter," according to which the tribulation includes not only the sufferings of Gospel heralds but also of those whose love will be chilled by the "antinomian heresy" (cf. 24:12).[150] He likewise regarded Matthew's expansion of the post-resurrection commission in 28:18 as designed to teach the convert to "observe all things," not to move him to repentence and faith.[151] Bacon noted some exception to this neo-legalism in the evangelist's description of Jesus' attitude toward the law. In his opinion, Matthew's account, in which Jesus subordinates but does not annul the law, is to be preferred to that of Mark.[152] In evidence, he referred to the Sermon on the Mount in which the legalist's expectation is "met to the ear" but "broken to the hope," the new requirement rendered so exorbitant that all mercenary righteousness collapses before it.[153]

For Bacon, the fact that Matthew's order admits scarcely any authority but Mark's, and thus gives primacy to Peter, was proof of the Gospel's Syrian provenance.[154] He located three instances of Matthew's embroidery on Mark's portrait of Peter in 14:28-33; 16:16-19 and 17:24-27. He described the first text as reflecting the final and most important item in the resurrection story, viz., Peter's "turning again" — the foundation of the resurrection faith.[155] In the second, he asserted that Matthew shares the position of the "Petrine" sections in Acts (chapters 1-15) on the issue of "distinctions of meats," and not the viewpoint of Luke who makes the compromise offered by James at the Apostolic Council the basis of settlement.[156] In the third and final passage, viewed as a later copy of the original Pauline claim to apostleship,[157] Peter's suggestion of Messiahship is made the foundation of the Church.[158]

Bacon stated that Matthew sometimes subordinated the *taxis* of Mark to his "pragmatic purpose," signalled in the rule "let all things be done unto edification."[159] This rule applied to Matthew's construction of chapters 8 and 9, as well as to his attempts to replace eastern, Quartodecimanian observance of Jesus' death by fitting his narrative to the western, hebdomadal system. Thus, despite its Syrian origin, the Gospel of Matthew reflected Roman, anti-Quartodecimanian observance of the passion and resurrection.[160]

Turning to Luke, Bacon wrote that the second-century tradition of Lukan authorship was reliable only insofar as it made the beloved physician "sponsor" of the Gospel in a general way.[161] He continued that the self-witness in 1:1ff. does not conflict with that ancient tradition, inasmuch as

Luke claims only to have heard the evangelic history recounted by its original preachers.[162] Bacon added that objections to his conclusions rested on arguments drawn from the "We" section of Acts, in which Luke appears as companion and collaborator of Paul.[163] These objections he sought to demolish by assigning the "We" sections to the companion of Paul or to Epaphroditus and by differentiating this Diarist from the final redactor.[164] The latter Bacon called the "Autor ad Theophilum" and described him as a post-apostolic Gentile Greek from Antioch, author of Luke 1:1-4, translator of Luke 1:5-2:52 and other fragments from the Hebrew, transcriber of most of the Greek Mark, translator of large portions of the Gospel from Aramaic and nearly the whole of "First Acts," and the revising editor of the appended Greek document or Diary underlying "Second Acts."[165]

C. C. Torrey had assigned the Gospel's composition to the year A.D. 60 or 61. He had assumed an early date for the Aramaic source underlying I Acts (ca. A.D. 44 or 45), and on the basis of the alleged homogeneity of II Acts had concluded that the volume was composed by Paul's companion during the apostle's lifetime. Bacon countered that the assumption of Aramaic priority over Greek in the early sources was unwarranted.[166] Conceding that the author of I Acts may have used the Diary in connection with events relating to Paul, he denied that the present form of II Acts is the work of the original Diarist, adding that in view of the unity of authorship the dual work should be assigned to the period of Domitian's reign.[167]

According to Bacon, Luke's "pragmatic" concern was in most respects identical with that of Matthew, i.e., directed toward a Syrian, Jewish-Christian and Petrine brotherhood. In evidence, Bacon referred to Luke's sharing Matthew's reaction to the Gnostic threat inherent in Mark's Christology[168] and to his bridging the gap between Markan adoptionism and the primitive Palestinian doctrine of human parentage by carrying Jesus' divine sonship back to his birth.[169] The corollary to this reaction, Bacon noted, lay in an anti-Baptist polemic, due to an association of the

Baptist's disciples with the Gnostic heresy.[170] As to the Gospel's birth and infancy narratives, Bacon wrote that what distinguished Luke from Matthew was his suggestion that though Jesus' birth was by the power of the Highest, Joseph might nevertheless have been his real father. On this belief the post-apostolic, "Pauline" idea of supernatural birth might later have been superimposed.[171] Luke further reflected his Jewish-Christian environment in the notion of divinity construed as apotheosis and in his concept of Jesus' sonship as essentially ethical and religious.[172]

The point at which Bacon believed Luke to be most unlike his predecessors and Paul in particular, was that of soteriology. Luke represented a "singular obscuration" of what Paul had set forth as the common gospel of Christ's death for man's sins.[173] The result, wrote Bacon, is that Luke's reiterated appeal to Isaiah 53 is always apologetic in character. In Luke, the death of the Servant is never connected with forgiveness,[174] and Jesus' exaltation is described as occurring in spite of the cross.[175] This "obscuration," Bacon thought, appears most clearly in Luke's Last Supper narrative, whose sole theme is the promise that the disciples will share in the Messianic banquet of the New Jerusalem,[176] a theme which Bacon traced to the Gospel's north-Syrian origin.[177] The reason for the obscuration Bacon located in Luke's aversion (shared with Matthew) to that antinomian transformation of the idea of vicarious retribution into a doctrine of the substitution of the innocent for the guilty, a dogma which could only result in moral laxity.[178]

According to Bacon, Luke displays a characteristically Jewish-Christian, Antiochene attitude toward the law, signalled in his treatment of the problem of Jewish- and Gentile-Christian fellowship in Acts. Luke's solution, wrote Bacon, serves the "double standard" promulgated by the "decrees" of Acts 15, and thus renders the compromise between Jew and Gentile offered by James at the apostolic "council" (not the Petrine approach as utilized by Matthew) the basis of settlement.[179] Bacon saw Luke's solution reflected in his elimination of the Markan "exile section,"[180] a solution totally out of harmony with that of Paul.[181] He thought he saw further evidence of Luke's reaction to the Pauline doctrine in his "Sermon" as well as in the Stephen narrative in Acts 7. In the "Sermon," God's grace is viewed as setting the standard for "thankworthy goodness." In Acts 7:38-42 Luke describes the "living oracles" as too ideal for Israel which subsequently appropriated the sacrificial system, God having abandoned her to a worship of the host of heaven — a far cry from the Pauline, cosmological idea.[182]

Bacon stated that despite Luke's failure to explain Peter's leadership of the Twelve,[183] or to give any datum from which to reckon the "forty days" in Acts 1:3,[184] the overall impression is of a two-volume work essentially Petrine.[185] He stated that the logion on "strengthening the brethren" in Luke 23:31f. makes Christ's appearance to Peter the basis for reassembling the scattered disciples following the crucifixion, a feature reflected in Luke's Midrashic treatment of Peter's Joppa vision, the purpose of which was to credit to Peter's account what had actually been the gospel of Paul.[186]

Bacon was certain that Redactor Luke shares with Matthew a western bias in his passion and resurrection narratives. But he was equally certain that Luke's narrative of the Last Supper, when freed of interpolation, best suits the Kiddush rather than the actual Passover meal, and thus reflects eastern, Quartodecimanian, pre-Pauline conception and practice.[187] Bacon summarized the reflections of ritual in Luke's dual work by stating that authentic Luke gives us precisely what we find in the liturgy of the North Syrian church of his time and cited the Didache ix as parallel.[188]

---

1. "Gospel Types in Primitive Tradition," p. 878; *Jesus The Son of God*, p. 27; *The Apostolic Message*, pp. 120, 124.
2. Cf. p. 23 above.
3. "The Purpose of Mark's Gospel," p. 50.
4. "The Matthaean Discourse in Parables, Mt. 13:1-52," *Journal of Biblical Literature*, XLVI (1927), p. 242.

5. *Is Mark a Roman Gospel?* p. 19.

6. *Jesus The Son of God*, p. 57; *The Apostolic Message*, p. 124; *The Beginnings of Gospel Story*, p. 152; *The Story of Jesus and the Beginnings of the Church*, p. 153.

7. *The Gospel of Mark, Its Composition and Date*, p. 306.

8. *The Development of the Synoptic Tradition*. A Study of the Composition, Sources and Interrelation of Matthew, Mark, Luke and Acts (unpublished: Yale University Divinity School, 1919), I, 102. Through the aid of a friend and admirer of Bacon, this unpublished manuscript was typed and given to the Yale library. The first draft was completed in 1919 and subsequently revised. Bacon considered it part of a series of "Modern Commentaries" on the historical books of the New Testament, of which *The Beginnings of Gospel Story* was the first and *Studies in Matthew* a surrogate for the second. Cf. the editor's note and preface together with *Studies in Matthew*, p. vii.

9. *The Development of the Synoptic Tradition*, p. 42.

10. *Ibid.*, pp. 58, 485.

11. *The Beginnings of Gospel Story*, p. xxi.

12. "The Resurrection in Judean and Galilean Tradition," *The Journal of Religion*, XI (1931), p. 507; *The Development of the Synoptic Tradition*, pp. 58, 167; *Jesus and Paul*, p. 13; "The Transfiguration Story: A Study of the Problem of the Sources of Our Synoptic Gospels," *The American Journal of Theology*, VI (1902), p. 249.

13. *Is Mark a Roman Gospel?* p. 87f.; "New and Old in Jesus' Relation to John," *Journal of Biblical Literature*, XLVIII (1929), p. 72; *The Story of Jesus and the Beginnings of the Church*, p. 257; "Jesus' Voice from Heaven," *The American Journal of Theology*, IX (1905), pp. 454, 471.

14. *The Development of the Synoptic Tradition*, p. 548.

15. *The Beginnings of Gospel Story*, p. 104.

16. *The Development of the Synoptic Tradition*, p. 42.

17. Bacon assumed a later editor in the composition of Mark 13. Though he most often referred to him as "Redactor Mark," because he did not limit the Gospel's development to two but to several stages, it is difficult to determine precisely what portion of the Gospel beyond its Petrine framework Bacon assigned to "R" or subsequent hands. Cf. "La date et l'origine de l'Evangile selon Marc," p. 285; "The Apocalyptic Chapter of the Synoptic Gospels," *Journal of Biblical Literature*, XXVIII (1909), p. 4; *The Development of the Synoptic Tradition*, pp. 489, 526f., 538; *The Beginnings of Gospel Story*, pp. x, xxi; "The Composition of Mark's Gospel," *The American Journal of Theology*, XIII (1909), p. 614.

18. "The 'Son' as Organ of Revelation," *The Harvard Theological Review*, IX (1916), pp. 382-85, 401; *The Beginnings of Gospel Story*, p. 48; cf. also "'Thankworthy' Goodness," *The Expositor*, VII (1914), pp. 509, 512.

19. "The Order of the Lukan 'Interpolations:' II. The Smaller Interpolation," p. 115, n. 4; *Is Mark a Roman Gospel?* p. 52; "The 'Son

of Man' in the Usage of Jesus," *Journal of Biblical Literature*, XLI
(1922), p. 155; *The Development of the Synoptic Tradition*, pp. 58,
105; *Studies in Matthew*, pp. xxv, 96; "The Prologue of Mark: A
Study of Sources and Structure," *Journal of Biblical Literature*,
XXVI (1907), p. 99.

20. "The Q Section on John the Baptist and the Shemoneh Esreh," pp. 23,
    27.
21. *The Development of the Synoptic Tradition*, p. 167.
22. *Ibid.*, p. 489.
23. "The Q Section on John the Baptist and the Shemoneh Esreh," p. 27;
    The Development of the Synoptic Tradition, p. 489.
24. *The Gospel of Mark*, p. 59f.
25. *Ibid.*, p. 60.
26. *The Development of the Synoptic Tradition*, p. 220.
27. "Peter's Triumph at Antioch," p. 211.
28. *The Development of the Synoptic Tradition*, p. 93.
29. "Why 'According to Matthew'?" *The Expositor*, XX (1920), pp. 296,
    304; "The Q Section on John the Baptist and the Shemoneh Esreh," p.
    27; *The Story of Jesus and the Beginnings of the Church*, p. 37. Earlier,
    Bacon had referred to the "Matthaean Logia" as underlying Luke's
    Gospel. His later conviction that Luke had no direct acquaintance
    with the Logia coincides with his rejection of the hypothesis of an
    Aramaic Matthew as a synoptic source. "S," consequently, came to
    replace the fictional Logia of Matthew as the second pillar in Bacon's
    synoptic theory. Cf. "What was the Sign of Jonah?" *The Biblical
    World*, XX (1902), p. 99; "Logia," *A Dictionary of Christ and the
    Gospels*, II, 48.
30. "The Redaction of Matthew 12," *Journal of Biblical Literature*, XLVI
    (1927), p. 47; "Why 'According to Matthew'?" p. 304; *Studies in
    Matthew*, p. 104; "The 'Order' of the Lukan 'Interpolations:' I.
    General Survey," *Journal of Biblical Literature*, XXXIV (1915), p.
    168f. Bacon's opinion was shared by the two Weisses, F. C. Burkitt
    and Prof. Vernon Bartlet, Cf. *Studies in Matthew*, p. 104.
31. "The Q Section on John the Baptist and the Shemoneh Esreh," p. 54;
    "The 'Order' of the Lukan Interpolations: III. The Longer
    Interpolation," *Journal of Biblical Literature*, XXXVII (1918), p. 20.
32. *Studies in Matthew*, p. 107.
33. *Ibid.*
34. *Ibid.*, p. 111; "The Q Section on John the Baptist and the Shemoneh
    Esreh," p. 30.
35. *Studies in Matthew*, p. 113.
36. "The 'Order' of the Lukan Interpolations: III. The Longer
    Interpolation," p. 20; "The Matthaean Discourse in Parables," p. 239;
    cf. "The Order of the Lukan 'Interpolations:' II. The Smaller
    Interpolation," p. 125.
37. "John as Preacher of Justification by Faith," pp. 182, 195; "The Q
    Section on John the Baptist and the Shemoneh Esreh," p. 54; *The
    Development of the Synoptic Tradition*, p. 527; "The Prologue of

Mark," p. 95; "Notes on the Gospel of Mark," *Journal of Biblical Literature*, XLII (1923), p. 138f.; "Pharisees and Herodians in Mark," *Journal of Biblical Literature*, XXIX (1920), p. 105f.; "New and Old in Jesus' Relation to John," p. 64. In Matthew 11:12-15, which Bacon maintained had its true context in the larger section of 21:23-46, he saw reflected the current Jewish legend of Elijah's function as exercising the power of the keys, a function later transferred to the Baptist. Cf. "Elias and the Men of Violence," *The Expositor*, VI (1902), pp. 33-35.

38. "The Nature and Design of Q," p. 688; "The 'Order' of the Lukan Interpolations. III. The Longer Interpolation," p. 27; "The Q Section on John the Baptist and the Shemoneh Esreh," p. 55; "John as Preacher of Justification by Faith," p. 193. Bacon asserted that the Son of Man in "S" is identical with the rejected Servant of Isaiah who works wonders not as signs of his own but of God's power. This, Bacon stated, contrasts with Mark's anachronistic application of the Son of Man title to situations where Jesus would simply have referred to himself as Servant. Cf. *The Story of Jesus and the Beginnings of the Church*, p. 268; "The New Testament Method of Differences," *The Hibbert Journal*, XXIII (1925), p. 450; "The Order of the Lukan 'Interpolations': II. The Smaller Interpolation," p. 127f.

39. "John as Preacher of Justification by Faith," p. 195.

40. "The 'Order' of the Lukan Interpolations: III. The Longer Interpolation," p. 47; "Jesus and the Law, A Study of the First 'Book' of Matthew," *Journal of Biblical Literature*, XLVII (1928), p. 221.

41. *Jesus and Paul*, p. 13f.; *The Story of Jesus and the Beginnings of the Church*, p. 181; cf. *The Beginnings of Gospel Story*, p. 48; "The Nature and Design of Q," p. 688.

42. *The Making of the New Testament*, pp. 136f., 144.

43. Bacon suggested that the Markan concept of the demons' recognition of the Christ may have been drawn from "S," and contended that "what Jesus really said, rests on the witness of the great S discourses." Cf. *The Beginnings of Gospel Story*, p. 18f.; *The Development of the Synoptic Tradition*, pp. 538, 541; *The Story of Jesus and the Beginnings of the Church*, p. 210.

44. "The Matthaean Discourse in Parables," p. 242f.; "The 'Order' of the Lukan 'Interpolations': I. General Survey," p. 171; "The Plaint of Wisdom in Matthew xxiii. 34-39," *The Expositor*, X (1915), p. 494; *The Development of the Synoptic Tradition*, p. 256; "The Redaction of Matthew 12," p. 24; "The Nature and Design of Q," p. 680; "The Q Section on John the Baptist and the Shemoneh Esreh," p. 23; *Studies in Matthew*, p. xxv.

45. "The Order of the Lukan 'Interpolations': II. The Smaller Interpolation," p. 125; *The Beginnings of Gospel Story*, p. xx, n. 5; *The Making of the New Testament*, p. 141.

46. *The Apostolic Message*, p. 296. Despite his admiration for Albert Schweitzer's *Geschichte der Leben-Jesu Forschung*, Bacon regretted that the volume showed so little first-hand knowledge of the sources recognized as the documentary basis for a critical history of Jesus,

writing that "Schweitzer has no more apprehension of the history, substance, and significance of Q, in distinction from later amplifications, than he thinks his opponents have of the fact that the canonical Gospels are products of their age," "A Turning Point in Synoptic Criticism," p. 64f.

47. "A Turning Point in Synoptic Criticism," p. 68.

48. "The Plaint of Wisdom in Matthew xxiii. 34-39," pp. 494, 508; "The 'Order' of the Lukan 'Interpolations': I. General Survey," p. 171; "The Order of the Lukan 'Interpolations': II. The Smaller Interpolation," p. 125.

49. "The Redaction of Matthew 12," p. 45.

50. *An Introduction to the New Testament*, p. 223; "Two Parables of Lost Opportunity," *The Hibbert Journal*, XXI (1923), p. 351.

51. "New and Old in Jesus' Relation to John," p. 64.

52. *Jesus The Son of God*, p. 98.

53. "The 'Son of Man' in the Usage of Jesus," p. 164; "The Plaint of Wisdom in Matthew xxiii. 34-39," p. 506.

54. *The Apostolic Message*, p. 296.

55. "The Order of the Lukan 'Interpolations': II. The Smaller Interpolation," p. 127f.; "The Nature and Design of Q," p. 688.

56. "Jesus and the Law," p. 221; "A Turning Point in Synoptic Criticism," p. 68.

57. "The 'Son of Man' in the Usage of Jesus," p. 162; "The Treatment of Mk. 6:14-8:26 in Luke," *Journal of Biblical Literature*, XXVI (1907), pp. 137, 145; "Jesus Christ," p. 166.

58. "The Prologue of Mark," p. 96f.; "Fig Tree," *A Dictionary of Christ and the Gospels*, I, 593.

59. *The Beginnings of Gospel Story*, p. xxi; *The Gospel of Mark*, p. 202.

60. *Studies in Matthew*, pp. xxv, 250.

61. *The Development of the Synoptic Tradition*, pp. 237, 245, 247.

62. "Genealogy of Jesus Christ," *A Dictionary of the Bible*, ed. James Hastings (New York: Charles Scribner's Sons, 1899), II, 140f.; *The Development of the Synoptic Tradition*, pp. 222, 232; *Studies in Matthew*, pp. 136, 138. Bacon posited an Ebionitic or Gnostic form of Matthew, according to which Jesus' birth was by human descent. This form, Bacon believed, was reflected in an "unassimilated" reading in the Sinaitic Syriac version ("Joseph begat Jesus who is called Christ"), a reading from which Irenaeus may have derived his application of the symbolism of Revelation 4:7 to the four Gospels, cf. "Critical Notes — Matthew and the Virgin Birth," *The American Journal of Theology*, XV (1911), p. 95.

63. *Studies in Matthew*, p. 250.

64. *The Development of the Synoptic Tradition*, p. 256; *Studies in Matthew*, pp. xxv, 96, 156.

65. *Studies in Matthew*, p. xxv. Bacon was loathe to credit Streeter with originating the Proto-Luke hypothesis, since he believed Streeter's arguments advanced but little the theories earlier developed by Paul

Feine in his *Eine Vorkanonische Überlieferung des Lukas in Evangelium und Apostelgeschichte.* Bacon insisted that Streeter's chief contribution to the hypothesis lay in his identification of the author of "L" with Paul's travel-companion. In his *Studies in Matthew*, Bacon wrote: "In view of the success attending his advocacy of the Proto-Lk theory it was natural that Canon Streeter should seek to merit more fully the title of originator by extending the same hypothesis to Mt.," p. 506.

66. "Jesus and the Law," p. 221.
67. *The Gospel of Mark*, p. 202.
68. *Studies in Matthew*, p. 113.
69. *Ibid.*, pp. xxv, 156; *The Development of the Synoptic Tradition*, p. 222.
70. "Genealogy of Jesus Christ," p. 141.
71. *Studies in Matthew*, pp. xxv, 96.
72. "The Chronological Scheme of Acts," p. 151; "Historico-Critical Analysis of the Book of Acts," p. 5; "The Redaction of Matthew 12," p. 47; "The Transfiguration Story," p. 265.
73. "The Chronological Scheme of Acts," p. 155; "More Philological Criticism of Acts," *The American Journal of Theology*, XXII (1918), p. 10.
74. "Some 'Western' Variants in the Text of Acts," p. 139. Bacon noted that the editors of *The Beginnings of Christianity* referred to his argument for Luke's transposition of his Petrine materials as "the point of most importance" for the rearrangement of Luke's sources, but expressed pique at the fact that the argument had been presented in mutilated form and all reference to him omitted. He further noted that his argument was subsequently noted without reference to the problem of the transposition. Bacon concluded that since in their principal discussion the editors of *Beginnings* had not mentioned any previous authority, the reader could only infer from such impersonal phrases as "it may be legitimate to suggest, etc." that the "suggestion" was the editors' own. Cf. "Wrath 'Unto the Uttermost,'" p. 374f., n. 2.
75. "Peter's Triumph at Antioch," p. 211; "More Philological Criticism of Acts," pp. 5, 10. Bacon's only qualification was that portions of the "Greek Acts of Paul" used in I Acts underwent a double process of translation into Aramaic and back into Greek. Cf. *The Development of the Synoptic Tradition*, p. 641f.; "Historico-Critical Analysis of the Book of Acts," p. 5.
76. "Stephen's Speech," p. 215f.
77. *The Development of the Synoptic Tradition*, p. 654; "The New Testament Method of Differences," p. 445; "Andronicus," p. 304.
78. *The Development of the Synoptic Tradition*, p. 657.
79. *Ibid.*, p. 665.
80. *Jesus The Son of God*, p. 11f.
81. *Is Mark a Roman Gospel?* pp. 29f., 33, 45; *The Gospel of Mark*, pp. 295, 304, 307.

82. *Studies in Matthew*, p. 67.

83. *The Gospel of Mark*, pp. 86, 131.

84. "The Apocalyptic Chapter of the Synoptic Gospels," pp. 18f., 23; *The Beginnings of Gospel Story*, p. 185.

85. "La date et l'origine de l'Evangile selon Marc," pp. 272f., 283f.; *The Beginnings of Gospel Story*, pp. 181, 183; *Is Mark a Roman Gospel?* p. 59; "The Apocalyptic Chapter of the Synoptic Gospels," p. 23f.

86. Toward the end of his life, Bacon assigned to the Gospel a date later than A.D. 75; cf. "La date et l'origine de l'Evangile selon Marc," p. 284.

87. *Is Mark a Roman Gospel?* p. 46.

88. *Ibid.*, pp. 13, 57; *The Development of the Synoptic Tradition*, pp. 17, 24.

89. "Gospel Types in Primitive Tradition," p. 878; *The Making of the New Testament*, p. 172; "The Purpose of Mark's Gospel," p. 53f.

90. *Jesus and Paul*, p. 16.

91. *Is Mark a Roman Gospel?* p. 88; *The Making of the New Testament*, p. 159.

92. *The Story of Jesus and the Beginnings of the Church*, p. 257; *Jesus The Son Of God or Primitive Christology*, p. 20f.

93. *Jesus and Paul*, pp. 167-169.

94. *The Making of the New Testament*, p. 162.

95. "The Treatment of Mk. 6:14-8:26 in Luke," p. 146; *Is Mark a Roman Gospel?* p. 69; *The Beginnings of Gospel Story*, p. xxiv.

96. *Jesus and Paul*, p. 116; *The Beginnings of Gospel Story*, p. 149. For Bacon, in the words of Johannes Weiss, a "Vervielfältigung eines historischen Vorgangs," "The Markan Theory of Demonic Recognition of the Christ," *Zeitschrift für die neutestamentliche Wissenschaft*, VI (1905), p. 154. Bacon stated that Wrede's notion that a theory of demonic recognition of the Messiah underlay Mark's account was incomplete, since it did not make larger allowance for the concrete, historic instance. He also expressed surprise at the choice Weiss had made among the Markan passages when selecting an original *historischer Vorgang*, asserting that the *Vorgang* in question was not to be found in Mark 1:24, but in the tradition underlying Matthew 8:23-24 = Mark 5:1-20, a passage which both Weiss and Wrede had dismissed as secondary; cf. *ibid.*, pp. 155f., 158.

97. *The Gospel of Mark*, p. 253.

98. *Is Mark a Roman Gospel?* p. 89; *The Story of Jesus and the Beginnings of the Church*, pp. 70f., 264; *The Beginnings of Gospel Story*, p. 175.

99. "The Gospel Paul 'Received'," p. 31.

100. "The Treatment of Mk. 6:14-8:26 in Luke," pp. 145, 149; *Is Mark a Roman Gospel?* p. 69f.; "Jesus and the Law," p. 221.

101. "The Order of the Lukan 'Interpolations': II. The Smaller Interpolation," p. 127f.; *Is Mark a Roman Gospel?* p. 70.

102. *The Beginnings of Gospel Story*, p. 88; "The Resurrection in Primitive Tradition and Observance," p. 394f.; "What was the 'Sign of Jonah'?" p. 111; *Is Mark a Roman Gospel?* pp. 69, 83.

103. *The Beginnings of Gospel Story*, p. 205.
104. *Ibid.*, p. 234; *The Making of the New Testament*, p. 170.
105. *The Beginnings of Gospel Story*, p. 235.
106. *Ibid.*, p. xix.
107. *Is Mark a Roman Gospel?* p. 77; "The Resurrection in Primitive Tradition and Observance," p. 396; *The Gospel of Mark*, p. 315.
108. *Jesus The Son of God*, p. 64, n. 8.
109. *The Beginnings of Gospel Story*, p. 235; "The Resurrection in Primitive Tradition and Observance," p. 396.
110. *Is Mark a Roman Gospel?* p. 77.
111. *The Making of the New Testament*, p. 172f.
112. "The Purpose of Mark's Gospel," p. 53; *The Story of Jesus and the Beginnings of the Church*, p. 148.
113. *The Beginnings of Gospel Story*, p. xxx; "The Resurrection in Primitive Tradition and Observance," p. 376; *Is Mark a Roman Gospel?* pp. 90, 96.
114. *The Beginnings of Gospel Story*, p. 217.
115. *The Making of the New Testament*, p. 173.
116. *Is Mark a Roman Gospel?* p. 96f.
117. *Jesus The Son of God*, p. 14.
118. *The Development of the Synoptic Tradition*, p. 40; *An Introduction to the New Testament*, pp. 44, 202; "Why 'According to Matthew'?" p. 296; *Jesus The Son of God*, p. 80; *The Making of the New Testament*, pp. 133, 135.
119. "Gospel Criticism and Christian Origins," *The American Journal of Theology*, VIII (1904), p. 616f.; *Jesus The Son of God*, p. 80; *Studies in Matthew*, p. 445.
120. "Why 'According to Matthew'?" p. 296.
121. *Studies in Matthew*, pp. 41, 46; "Why 'According to Matthew'?" pp. 307ff.; *The Development of the Synoptic Tradition*, pp. 161, 175, 177; *Is Mark a Roman Gospel?* p. 12. In a review of Bacon's *Studies in Matthew*, Burton Scott Easton had criticized Bacon's suggestion that "Matthew" may have been a primitive Christian totally unknown to us. In reply, Bacon asserted that this possibility had been introduced merely to cover all eventualities, and that it was shortly after dismissed as less probable than the transference theory, cf. "A Review Reviewed," *Anglican Theological Review*, XII (1931), pp. 212f., 214.
122. "Are the 'New Sayings of Christ' Authentic?" *The Outlook*, LVI (1897), pp. 785, 787; "Date and Habitat of the Elders of Papias," *Zeitschrift für die neutestamentliche Wissenschaft*, XII (1911), p. 186; *The Sermon on the Mount*, Its Literary Structure and Didactic Purpose (New York: Macmillan and Co., 1902), pp. 3f., 27; "What was the 'Sign of Jonah'?" p. 99; "Chips from the Workshop of the Evangelists," *The Independent*, LVI (1904), p. 1495; "Logia," p. 49; *The Fourth Gospel in Research and Debate*, pp. 9, 286; "Jesus Christ," p. 163.

123. "Why Callest Thou Me Good?" *The Biblical World*, VI (1895), p. 340; *An Introduction to the New Testament*, p. 197; *The Making of the New Testament*, p. 151. Bacon earlier posited three stages in the Gospel's development — an Aramaic followed by two Greek editions. Assigning the combination of the *logia* with Peter's memorabilia as taken down by Mark to edition number two, he described it as resembling the Gospel of the Nazarenes in use among Aramaic-speaking Christians of Aleppo, not necessarily written nor accessible only to Matthew. From this we may assume that according to Bacon's earlier as well as his revised theory, further use and combination of sources were to be assigned to the final editor. For Bacon, then, the name "Matthew" represented the final redactor. Cf. *The Making of the New Testament*, pp. 135, 151; "Jesus and the Law," p. 206f.; *Studies in Matthew*, pp. xxv, 113; *The Sermon on the Mount*, p. 170.

124. "Are the 'New Sayings of Christ' Authentic?" p. 787f.

125. *Studies in Matthew*, pp. xi, xiii.

126. *The Development of the Synoptic Tradition*, p. 141.

127. *The Gospel of Mark*, pp. 102-04.

128. "La date et l'origine de l'Evangile selon Marc," p. 285.

129. *Studies in Matthew*, pp. 67, 69.

130. "La date et l'origine de l'Evangile selon Marc," p. 282.

131. *Studies in Matthew*, p. 76.

132. *Ibid.*, p. 23.

133. *Ibid.*, pp. 35, 38.

134. "As to the Canonization of Matthew," *The Harvard Theological Review*, XXII (1929), p. 173.

135. "The Gospel Stories of the Virgin Birth," *The Independent*, LV (1903), p. 3038; *Is Mark a Roman Gospel?* p. 72.

136. *Is Mark a Roman Gospel?* p. 72.

137. *Studies in Matthew*, p. 421; "The 'Son of Man' in the Usage of Jesus," p. 169f.; "Jesus and the Law," p. 216.

138. "The Markan Theory of Demonic Recognition of the Christ," p. 155; *The Beginnings of Gospel Story*, p. 17; "The Gospel Paul 'Received'," pp. 31, 37.

139. "A Turning Point in Synoptic Criticism," p. 69; *Studies in Matthew*, p. 413.

140. "Jesus and the Law," p. 208f.; *Jesus and Paul*, p. 2; *The Sermon on the Mount*, p. 106.

141. "The 'Five Books' of Matthew versus the Jews," *The Expositor*, XV (1918), pp. 60, 66; *The Sermon on the Mount*, p. 168; "The Nature and Design of Q," p. 676.

142. Regarding this "second book," Bacon, as Hawkins, was reminded of the enumerations in Pirke Aboth, and spoke of it as a striking instance of Matthew's "pragmatic use of history," cf. The 'Order' of the Lukan 'Interpolations:' I. General Survey, p. 176; *Studies in Matthew*, pp. 187ff.

143. *Studies in Matthew*, pp. 202, 219.

144. "The 'Order' of the Lukan 'Interpolations': I. General Survey," p. 176.
145. "The Matthaean Discourse in Parables," p. 238; *Studies in Matthew*, p. 107.
146. Bacon's contention that "order" for Matthew consisted in a five-fold arrangement of commandments led him to assert that a sixteenth century paper manuscript discovered in the monastery of Iveran on Mount Athos and catalogued as a compend in five books against the Jews by "Matthew a monk," a work which J. Rendel Harris and F. C. Burkitt assumed comprised that book of testimonies described by Papias as the "Logia," was none other than our canonical Matthew, cf. "The 'Five Books' of Matthew versus the Jews," pp. 56, 60, 62, 66.
147. *Jesus and Paul*, p. 2.
148. "'Thankworthy' Goodness," pp. 505, 507.
149. "Why Callest Thou Me Good?" p. 341f.
150. *The Development of the Synoptic Tradition*, p. 321; "Two Parables of Lost Opportunity," p. 348.
151. "Is Baptism Syncretistic?" p. 162; *Jesus The Son Of God or Primitive Christology*, p. 9; "The Jesus of History and the Christ of Religion," p. 216.
152. *Studies in Matthew*, p. 354.
153. "The Blessing of the Peacemakers," *The Expository Times*, XLI (1929), p. 60; *The Sermon on the Mount*, pp. 107-09.
154. "A Turning Point in Synoptic Criticism," p. 69; *Studies in Matthew*, p. 229.
155. "The Petrine Supplements of Matthew," *The Expositor*, XIII (1917), pp. 3, 8, 11, 16; *Studies in Matthew*, p. 223.
     Studies in Matthew, p. 224.
157. "Jesus Christ," pp. 160, 166; "The Petrine Supplements of Matthew," p. 11f.
158. "Jesus Christ," p. 166. When Julius Grill attempted to account for Matthew's embellishments in terms of Roman influence during the time of St. Victor, Bacon sputtered that he "must be regarded as under some temporary hallucination," "The Petrine Supplements of Matthew," p. 3.
159. "Editorial Arrangement in Matthew VIII.-IX," *The Expositor*, XIX (1920), p. 218.
160. "The Resurrection in Primitive Tradition and Observance," pp. 376, 394f.
161. *The Development of the Synoptic Tradition*, pp. 600, 613.
162. Not as told by the apostles, as Justin and Irenaeus had erroneously inferred. Cf. "Le temoignage de Luc sur lui-meme," *Revue d'Histoire et de Philosophie Religieuses*, VIII (1928), pp. 222f., 226.
163. *Ibid.*, p. 226.
164. *An Introduction to the New Testament*, p. 211, n. 4. Cf. "Historico-Critical Analysis of the Book of Acts," p. 8, in which Bacon allows for the possibility that the Diarist is also the author of final Luke-Acts, though he admits the objections to such a theory cannot be taken

lightly. This essay is undated, but can be assigned to an early period since it does not reflect Bacon's maturer view.

165. "More Philological Criticism of Acts," pp. 7, 10, 20; "Eagle and Basket on the Antioch Chalice," p. 5.

166. *The Gospel of the Hellenists*, p. 121. Of Torrey (and C. F. Burney, who shared the latter's views) Bacon wrote, "translation Greek is to them a key not to some, but *all* the problems of the Gospel. It is the panacea which makes further inquiry needless. Reproduce the 'original Aramaic,' plead Burney and Torrey, and there is little or no more occasion for higher criticism."

167. "More Philological Criticism of Acts," pp. 7ff.

168. "The Gospel Stories of the Virgin Birth," p. 3037f.

169. *Ibid.*; *Is Mark a Roman Gospel?* p. 89; *The Story of Jesus and the Beginnings of the Church*, p. 70; "Gospel Types in Primitive Tradition," p. 895.

170. "New and Old in Jesus' Relation to John," pp. 44f., 50, 66, 80.

171. "Genealogy of Jesus Christ," p. 140; "The Gospel Stories of the Virgin Birth," p. 3037; *The Development of the Synoptic Tradition*, p. 57; "The Supernatural Birth of Jesus," p. 8.

172. "The Gospel Stories of the Virgin Birth," p. 3038; "Jesus as Lord," *The Harvard Theological Review*, IV (1911), p. 210f.; *Jesus The Son Of God or Primitive Christology*, p. 81; *Jesus The Son of God*, p. 19.

173. "The New Testament Method of Differences," p. 448; *Jesus and Paul*, p. 116; *The Apostolic Message*, p. 271.

174. "The Gospel Paul 'Received'," p. 31; *The Apostolic Message*, p. 259.

175. "The New Testament Method of Differences," p. 451.

176. *The Apostolic Message*, p. 269; *The Gospel of Mark*, p. 180; "The Lukan Tradition of the Lord's Supper," *The Harvard Theological Review,* V (1912), p. 339f.

177. *The Apostolic Message*, p. 271.

178. "The Gospel Paul 'Received'," p. 37; Jesus and the Law," p. 218; *Jesus and Paul*, p. 116; "Two Parables of Lost Opportunity," p. 338.

179. "More Philological Criticism of Acts," p. 22; *Studies in Matthew*, p. 224.

180. *The Story of Jesus and the Beginnings of the Church*, p. 118.

181. "Le temoignage de Luc sur lui-meme," p. 225.

182. "'Thankworthy' Goodness," p. 507; "Stephen's Speech," pp. 226, 245, 254, 258, 264.

183. "Papias and the Gospel According to the Hebrews," *The Expositor*, XI (1905), p. 172f.; *The Founding of the Church, Modern Religious Problems*, ed. Ambrose White Vernon (Boston: Houghton, Mifflin and Co., 1909), p. 31.

184. "The Resurrection in Primitive Tradition and Observance," p. 402.

185. "The New Testament Method of Differences," p. 448; cf. *The Story of St. Paul*, p. 82.

186. *The Story of Jesus and the Beginnings of the Church*, p. 296; *The*

Development of the Synoptic Tradition, p. 548; "Immortality in the Fourth Gospel," pp. 270, 281, 283; "The Mystical Experience of St. Paul," p. 96.

187. "The Lukan Tradition of the Lord's Supper," pp. 340-44.
188. "The New Testament Method of Differences," p. 452; "Eagle and Basket on the Antioch Chalice," p. 3.

CHAPTER FIVE
THE EPHESIAN SYNTHESIS

I: *"What Entered the Heart of Man" — The Johannine Literature*:

Bacon described the Fourth Gospel and Johannine epistles as a synthesis of the Galilean and Pauline Gospels via Hellenistic individualism and mysticism; fixed the Johannine literature under the rubric "what entered the heart of man,"[1] and advanced to the discussion of authorship by rejecting the traditional views. He stated that the notion of direct apostolic authorship was a later development, originating with Irenaeus who had erroneously included John of Zebedee among Papias' informants and thus transferred the Johannine tradition from Jerusalem to Asia.[2] This fallacious testimony, Bacon contended, extended the life-time of the apostle to the reign of Domitian, so as to assign him the Book of Revelation as well as the four "anonymous" Ephesian writings.[3] Stating as his final position that the Gospel had attained its present form prior to A.D. 154,[4] Bacon concluded that the idea of its Zebedean authorship was dependent on the alleged apostolic authorship of Revelation, a notion which in turn constituted a misinterpretation of the device of impersonation common to apocalyptic literature.[5]

In opposition to Zahn and von Harnack who believed that the Fourth Gospel was composed by the "elder John of Ephesus," disciple of the apostle and leader of Asiatic Christendom, Bacon noted the absence of any reference to an Ephesian "elder" in writings of the period A.D. 70-250.[6] He suggested that this elder, conceivably one of Papias' informants, might have penned the Apocalypse.[7] Indeed, given the transference of Johannine tradition to Asia (Ephesus), the traits and authorship of this informant could be assigned to Zahn's and von Harnack's mythical "elder." In light of these observations, Bacon concluded that the only elder capable of identification was John of Jerusalem, the pseudo-John of Ephesus a mere "hydra-headed" invention leaping "full panoplied from the teeming brain of Harnack."[8]

Early on, Bacon had suggested that the witness of the Zebedee might underlie the original form of the Fourth Gospel and concluded for a common authorship of the Gospel (at least in substance) and the three epistles.[9] He accordingly attributed the Gospel minus the appendix to the nameless elder of Ephesus, whom he called "Theologos," "Strateas" or "A" (in contrast to the Redactor, "R"), a successor to Paul or Apollos at Ephesus at the close of the first century, and whom Papias included with the Elder John of Jerusalem among his informants.[10] In order to secure a hearing this anonymous writer created a sponsor for his Gospel in the person of the "beloved disciple."[11]

If, in Bacon's opinion, the original author's purpose was to gain an audience, the redactor's aim was to secure canonicity for the Gospel in its final form.[12] For this reason, Bacon contended, "R" not only identified the "beloved disciple" with the son of Zebedee, but also with the evangelist himself, and thus imposed on the latter the mask of apostolicity.[13] The price which the redactor had to pay for his volume's admission to the canon was to round off his Asiatic, Pauline Gospel with an appendix, in which Peter received the status of shepherd or administrator (21:15-19), in contrast to that of John, the "teaching" elder.[14] The epilogue's chief object, however, was to commend still another authority, that of the Gospel itself which repeatedly sets over against Peter a mysterious, unnamed figure.[15] Bacon stated that the identification of this figure with the son of Zebedee and the evangelist was not outright. Rather, the redactor placed responsibility for the identification with his readers, and by rendering Jesus' answer to Peter in 21:21ff. sufficiently vague, met the conflicting traditions concerning the Zebedee's fate by suggesting that John's "tarrying" consisted not in physical survival, but in an abiding witness.[16]

II. *The Johannine Sources*:

In his early Johannine studies, Bacon agreed that the Gospel reflected a composite origin, and suggested the original author had readjusted a source relating John's call to discipleship in order to commend it to a church oriented to Petrine tradition.[17] He later abandoned this theory, stating that the free handling of synoptic themes in the interest of apologetic sufficiently accounted for divergence from synoptic tradition.[18] In Bacon's mature view, the Gospel reflected three stages of development. The first consisted of a combination of "festal discourses" appropriate to feasts of the Jewish year, each discourse introduced by its appropriate "sign." This combination Bacon confidently assigned to the "elder-evangelist."[19] The second stage comprised an expansion of the discourses into a narrative of the life of Christ — also the work of the "elder," at least in its original form.[20] Responsibility for the final stage Bacon assigned to the redactor, who superimposed distinctively Pauline material on his exemplar and made it his chief concern to accomodate John to the synoptic pattern.[21]

III. *The Plan and Theology of the Fourth Gospel*:

According to Bacon, the basic plan of the Gospel in its final form consists in a series of discourses introduced by a "sign" and adapted to feasts of the Mosaic calendar.[22] He continued that the Fourth Gospel, just as the synoptics, focuses on the themes of new birth and justification, first struck in Jesus' dialogue with Nicodemus.[23] The result of this position is that both the Synoptists and John are made historically and theologically dependent upon Paul or his Hellenistic predecessors. In his posthumously published work on the Fourth Gospel, however, Bacon contended that Paul was relatively unimportant to that body of tradition to which the "Elder" testifies.[24] In light of this contention, Bacon's earlier reference to the Gospel as giving "absolute loyalty to Paulinism" or to the Fourth Evangelist as the great "vindicator" of Paul,[25] requires modification. But there is little if any indication that Bacon altered his view prior to

The Gospel of the Hellenists. For this reason, his main argument is presented here on the assumption it would have suffered little radical adjustment.

In opposition to F. C. Baur, Bacon maintained that rapprochement between the contending parties in primitive Christianity had been begun by Paul, but that the "greater and deeper work" had been done by the nameless Ephesian "Elder."[26] He had achieved a higher unity, allowing for both Semitic and Hellenistic conceptions, and it was precisely such a unity that became the basis of Christianity as a new world-religion.[27] With these provisos, Bacon agreed with Baur that the immediate occasion for the reconciliation was the Gnostic threat and described the Ephesian evangelist as wrestling for catholic doctrine against Gnosticizing "adversaries."[28]

The Christology of the Fourth Gospel thus constituted a synthesis of the primitive doctrine of Jesus as Servant and the Hellenistic doctrine of the Incarnation.[29] Writing that the Fourth Evangelist counteracts ultra-Pauline, docetic dualism by accenting the reality of Jesus' birth, death and resurrection,[30] Bacon described the Gospel as reflecting historical superiority over the synoptics.[31] For example, the Fourth Evangelist was loyal to an "older tradition" according to which Jesus attained the age of Rabbi when he began his ministry, his birth thus occurring forty to forty-nine years prior to his public appearance.[32] The Gospel's geography, which effected an extraordinary reversal of synoptic setting by locating the Baptist's activity in Transjordan and Samaria and by prefixing to the story of Jesus' public ministry a new, pre-Galilean or Samaritan ministry, reflected a certain accuracy.[33] The evangelist's conviction, shared with early heresiologues, was that the original seat of Gnostic heresy lay at Samaria. For this reason, his eagerness to strike at the taproot of Gnosticism by correcting exaggerated preference for the Baptist influenced his location of the beginning of Jesus' work.[34] But, Bacon asserted, the evangelist's reasons for this radical departure went beyond those of mere literary convenience or apologetic.[35] For if the locale from which the Baptist's

disciples finally came to swell the ranks was the area beyond
Jordan, then Samaria, to which those "Hellenistic refugees"
had fled after the murder of Stephen, was the heartland of
Gnosticism, an area "acutely" Hellenized by the followers of
Simon of Gitta and Menander.[36]

Bacon arrived at a similar conclusion regarding the
Gospel's chronology. He contended that the Gospel's
scheme of festal journeys ought not be undervalued since
even an "artificial" scheme could be built upon sound
tradition.[37] This was true, e.g., of chapter 11, which he
believed preserved a sense of the "primitive values" which
otherwise would scarcely have survived,[38] and it was true,
above all, of the Gospel's correction of the Lukan dating of
the crucifixion. Bacon not merely allowed the possibility
that Jesus died on Nisan 14, but assigned that date historical
superiority. He insisted that sufficient traces remained in all
three synoptic Gospels to prove that the passion narrative in
its pre-canonical form agreed with Johannine tradition and
with the practice of eastern churches which annually
commemorated the death and resurrection on Nisan 14, an
observance sanctioned and approved by Paul himself.[39]

For Bacon, this emphatically historical aspect of the
Gospel was synthesized with what von Harnack had termed
the "sacramentarian gospel of the mystagogue."[40] Such had
its background in what Bacon described as a "lyric Gnosis"
in which a high Christology employing Stoic concepts
mingled more or less incongruously with Rabbinic
mythology.[41] Following Bacon's change of view with respect
to the Gospel's dependence upon Pauline thought,[42] this
feature was no longer assigned to Paul but to his
predecessors. But early or late, Bacon regarded the
transition from the Semitic "Word" to the Logos of
Hellenism as easy once that "Word" had been identified with
the divine Wisdom.[43] What resulted, of course, was that
Bacon rendered the Fourth Evangelist independent of Paul
and made both equally dependent on those "refugees" who
were the true founders of the Gentile mission and whose
struggles with their Samaritan neighbors provided the basis
for the Incarnation doctrine.

At one point Bacon early distanced the Fourth Gospel from Paul — at the point of its "restatement" of the Church's doctrine of eschatology.[44] By its "emancipation from the sinister inheritance of late-Jewish apocalyptic,"[45] the Gospel effected that "complete transfer" of emphasis from an apocalyptic type judgment toward a judgment already executed in the coming of Jesus and the Spirit. Early assigning and later denying to Paul the stimulus for such transfer, Bacon fixed the transfer itself in the Gospel's concept of mystical union with the eternal Christ.[46] With the "Elder," then, the Greek view of immortality had "triumphed" over the Jewish idea of resurrection.[47]

In the area of law as well, Bacon described the Fourth Gospel as the "supreme synthetic factor."[48] To the Petrine, social-ethical concept as well as to the commandment of love reflected in the Sayings Source, the evangelist-elder wedded a view of salvation attained by moral assimilation to the mind of Christ.[49] Loyal to both conceptions, the Gospel achieved this synthesis by appropriating from the mystery cults the idea of redemption through mystical union with the divine.[50] Thus, the Johannine doctrine of life via "transfusion of the Spirit" counteracted the earlier, "Jewish" eschatology and furnished the antidote to the "crudities" of Jewish legalism.[51]

In matters of ritual, Bacon noted the evangelist's treatment of the Eucharistic materials as reflecting his overall attempt at synthesis. He pointed first to the author's joining Paul's understanding of the Supper to the "Galilean" rite of the breaking of bread by attaching a Quartodecimanian interpretation to the feeding of the multitude in chapter 6.[52] He then referred to the evangelist's substitution of the rite of purification for the Eucharist as a Last Supper or Kiddush.[53] Contending that I Corinthians 11:23-25 gave the "ultimate record of fact," Bacon located the rationale for this "strange substitution" in the evangelist's Hellenistic concept of the "hour" of Jesus' "lifting up" as the Passover of God. From this standpoint, the eve of "Passover" constituted the Church's preparation, to which one theme alone was appropriate — that of the bride's purification, symbolized in the washing of feet.

Thus, for Bacon, the New Testament constituted the adjustment of two religious concepts. The one he described as Asiatic, Aryan, Western, Hellenistic, Gentile, universalistic, individual-mystical, preoccupied with the "aeonian Christ, emphasizing destiny, and its goal personal immortality."[54] The other he termed Semitic, Galilean, particularistic, social, ethical, preoccupied with the historical Jesus, emphasizing duty, and its goal the Kingdom of God. The one he called the "gospel about Jesus," reflected in the letters of Paul and the Johannine literature, and the other the "Petrine" gospel or "gospel of Jesus," broadly reflected in the apotheosis Christology of the Synoptists and in the higher and better morality exemplified in Matthew's Sermon. Both conceptions, Bacon argued, were justified in claiming to emanate from Jesus. Neither without the other could fully claim to represent his spirit and life.[55] Bacon hence saw the development of Christianity as continuous, not disjunctive, and by the perfection of this adjustment, he concluded, Christianity had proved its right to be the "ultimate world-religion."[56]

IV. *The Post-Apostolic Age*:

According to Bacon, the delicate balance between the "gospel of" and "about Jesus" was not maintained following the New Testament age. Portions of the church, confronted with Gnosticism, antinomianism and Docetism, fell back upon the tradition of the "apostles and elders."[57] As a result, apostolic and quasi-apostolic literature gained increasing authority.[58] In this period, Bacon stated, the "Word of the Lord," "the commandments of the apostles" and even the "revelations of the prophets" ceased to be living realities and were crystallized into written form.[59] Even in the heart of the Pauline mission, the gospel of conscious revelation and inspiration had degenerated into the "hum-drum levels of mere 'catholic' catechetics."[60] Bacon described this reaction as "legalistic," "materialistic" and synagogal, a reaction severe enough to render Paul's gospel impossible of being heard without accomodation to Petrine tradition.[61] He believed the Epistle of James gave preeminent expression to this reaction, with its doctrine of the "higher law."[62] But, he asserted, it was not Paul's doctrine as such which evoked James' protest, but rather a type of ultra-Pauline intellectualism to which the Epistle to the Hebrews gave the most eloquent expression.[63]

Bacon concluded that in face of the two extremes of Jewish-Christianity and radical ultra-Paulinism, the central body of the Church, under pressure of imperial persecution and faced with the peril of Gnosticism, was driven to a rapprochement between "those of Peter and of Paul."[64] This central body felt its way toward a faith which retained values from both sides and left the results to future generations.[65] When effort at unity succeeded, culminating in the Council of Nicea, Roman practice as reflected in synoptic tradition was combined with the Asian and Johannine.[66] The First Epistle of Peter constituted the "first great irenicon" of this rapprochement.[67]

---

1. *Jesus The Son of God*, p. 15.
2. "Recent Aspects of the Johannine Problem: I. The External Evidence," *The Hibbert Journal*, I (1903), p. 530f.; "The Elder John in Jerusalem," *Zeitschrift für die neutestamentliche Wissenschaft*, XXVI (1927), pp. 197, 199; "An Emendation of the Papias Fragment," *Journal of Biblical Literature*, XVII (1898), pp. 176, 178, 181; "The Elder of Ephesus and the Elder John," *The Hibbert Journal*, XXVI (1927), p. 125; "Gospel Criticism and Christian Origins," p. 619; "The Elder John, Papias, Irenaeus, Eusebius and the Syriac Translator," *Journal of Biblical Literature*, XVII (1908), pp. 8, 15, 19ff.; "Papias and the Gospel According to the Hebrews," p. 176f.; "Papias," *The New Schaff-Herzog Encyclopedia of Religious Knowledge*, VIII, 339f.; "Date and Habitat of the Elders of Papias," p. 187; "John and the Pseudo-Johne," *Sonderabdruck aus der Zeitschrift für die neutestamentliche Wissenschaft und die Kunde der älteren Kirche* (Giessen: A. Töpelmann, 1932), 31. Band, Heft 2, p. 149. (This essay was the last to come from Bacon's pen).
3. *The Gospel of the Hellenists*, p. 421; "The Elder John in Jerusalem," p. 199.
4. "The Motivation of John 21:15-25," p. 79. In his *Fourth Gospel in Research and Debate*, Bacon had assumed a later date for the final form of the Gospel; cf. *Studies in Matthew*, p. 466.

5. *The Gospel of the Hellenists*, p. 24; *An Introduction to the New Testament*, pp. 246ff. (a volume in which Bacon still supported the Zebedean authorship of Revelation, cf. pp. 231ff.).

6. "The Mythical 'Elder John' of Ephesus," *The Hibbert Journal*, XXIX (1931), pp. 313-15.

7. "Date and Habitat of the Elders of Papias," pp. 182, 187; "Chips from the Workshop of the Evangelists," p. 1495; "The 'Defence' of the Fourth Gospel," *The Hibbert Journal*, VI (1907), p. 124f.

8. "Papias and the Gospel According to the Hebrews," p. 176; "The Elder John in Jerusalem," p. 194; "Johannes Redivivus," *The Journal of Religion*, XI (1931), pp. 223, 238; "In My Father's House are Many Mansions," *The Expository Times*, XLIII (1931), p. 478; "The Johannine Problem," *The Independent*, LVII (1904), p. 325; "The Mythical 'Elder John' of Ephesus," p. 313; "Primitive Christianity," p. 763.

9. *An Introduction to the New Testament*, pp. 246, 252, 268, 270f.; "The 'Defence' of the Fourth Gospel," p. 124f.; "The 'Other' Comforter," p. 276; *The Gospel of the Hellenists*, pp. 45, 365; "In My Father's House are Many Mansions," p. 478; "Enter the Higher Criticism," p. 47; *The Fourth Gospel in Research and Debate*, p. 269.

10. *The Fourth Gospel in Research and Debate*, pp. 193, 209, 269, 308, 453f.; "The Johannine Problem," p. 339; "The 'Defence' of the Fourth Gospel," pp. 124, 133; "The Mythical 'Elder John' of Ephesus," p. 326; "The Elder of Ephesus and the Elder John," p. 116; "In My Father's House are Many Mansions," p. 478; *An Introduction to the New Testament*, p. 248; "Enter the Higher Criticism," p. 47. In his volume, *Criticism of the Fourth Gospel*, William Sanday had erroneously stated that Bacon had ascribed the main body of the Gospel to John the Presbyter, and had assigned another author to the First Epistle. Bacon twice took umbrage at this error, in the second instance noting that Prof. Sanday had expressed his regret at the unintentional misrepresentation. Cf. *The Fourth Gospel in Research and Debate*, pp. 189, 444. Bacon referred a third time to Sanday's error in "The 'Other' Comforter," p. 276, n. 1. J. Estlin Carpenter's statement that Bacon persisted as late as 1925 in his identification of the elder with the John of Eusebius (Papias) was, Bacon said, a misunderstanding — the Ephesian elder mentioned in II and III John, and no doubt connected with the First Epistle and Gospel, "had nothing in common with the Elder John of Papias save the title of 'Elder' "; cf. "The Elder of Ephesus and the Elder John," p. 116.

11. *The Fourth Gospel in Research and Debate*, p. 308f.

12. *Ibid.*, p. 219.

13. *Ibid.*, pp. 209, 219, 308f., 454; "The 'Defence' of the Fourth Gospel," p. 124f.; "John and the Pseudo-Johns," p. 149; "Enter the Higher Criticism," p. 47.

14. "The Motivation of John 21:15-25," p. 73f.

15. *The Making of the New Testament*, p. 242f.

16. "The Martyr Apostles," *The Expositor*, IV (1907), p. 238f. For Bacon's discussion of the authorship of Revelation, which he regarded as intimately connected with the question of the Johannine authorship of the Gospel and epistles, cf. "The Latin Prologues of John," *Journal of Biblical Literature*, XXXII (1913), p. 216f.; "Adhuc in Corpore Constituto," *The Harvard Theological Review*, XXIII (1930), p. 305f.; "Marcion, Papias, and 'The Elders'," *The Journal of Theological Studies*, XXIII (1922), pp. 139, 144f., 156f., 159; "The Anti-Marcionite Prologue to John," *Journal of Biblical Literature*, XLIX (1930), pp. 43f., 46f., 49f.; *Studies in Matthew*, pp. 463, 452ff.; *An Introduction to the New Testament*, pp. vi, 231f., 238, 275; "The Authoress of Revelation — A Conjecture," *The Harvard Theological Review*, XXIII (1930), pp. 235, 240, 244f., 247, 248f.; "The Martyr Apostles," pp. 236f., 252; "Johannes Redivivus," pp. 224, 226, 228f., 233f., 241; "John and the Pseudo-Johns," pp. 138f., 144; *The Making of the New Testament*, p. 199; "The Elder John, Papias, Irenaeus, Eusebius and the Syriac Translator," pp. 4f., 8; *The Fourth Gospel in Research and Debate*, pp. 171, 181f.

17. "Recent Aspects of the Johannine Problem: III. Indirect Internal Evidence," p. 373f.

18. "Sources and Method of the Fourth Evangelist," *The Hibbert Journal*, XXV (1926), p. 129.

19. *The Gospel of the Hellenists*, p. 138.

20. *Ibid.*, p. 139.

21. "Pauline Elements in the Fourth Gospel. I. A Study of John i-iv," *Anglican Theological Review*, XI (1929), p. 223; *The Gospel of the Hellenists*, p. 140.

22. *An Introduction to the New Testament*, p. 258; "After Six Days: A New Clue for Gospel Critics," *The Harvard Theological Review*, VIII (1915), p. 103.

23. "Pauline Elements in the Fourth Gospel," p. 208f.

24. *The Gospel of the Hellenists*, pp. 58ff.

25. *The Fourth Gospel in Research and Debate*, p. 281; *He Opened To Us The Scriptures*, p. 100.

26. "A Century of Change in New Testament Criticism," p. 622.

27. "The Relations of New Testament Science to Kindred Sciences," p. 579; "A Century of Change in New Testament Criticism," p. 621.

28. "Enter the Higher Criticism," p. 47. Cf. *Jesus and Paul*, p. 203; "The 'Defence' of the Fourth Gospel," p. 136.

29. "Two Forgotten Creeds," *The Harvard Theological Review*, VI (1913), p. 294.

30. *The Fourth Gospel in Research and Debate*, p. 288.

31. *Jesus and Paul*, p. 126; "Ultimate Problems of Biblical Science," p. 6.

32. "Lukan versus Johannine Chronology," *The Expositor*, III (1907), p. 219; "Notes on Gospel Chronology," *Journal of Biblical Literature*, XXVIII (1909), p. 148.

33. "Is Baptism Syncretistic?" p. 171; "History and Dogma in John," *The Hibbert Journal*, XXVIII (1929), p. 114.

34. "New and Old in Jesus' Relation to John," p. 52f.; "Pauline Elements in the Fourth Gospel. I," p. 222.
35. "History and Dogma in John," p. 123f.
36. *The Gospel of the Hellenists*, pp, 80, 86, 89.
37. "History and Dogma in John," p. 123.
38. "The Festival of Lives Given for the Nation in Jewish and Christian Faith," p. 278.
39. "The Resurrection in Primitive Tradition and Observance," p. 376; cf. also pp. 400, 402f.
40. "Gospel Types in Primitive Tradition," p. 888.
41. *The Gospel of the Hellenists*, p. 383.
42. Cf. p. 62f. above.
43. *The Gospel of the Hellenists*, p. 149f.
44. *Jesus and Paul*, p. 206.
45. *Jesus The Son of God*, p. 135.
46. *The Gospel of the Hellenists*, p. 181.
47. "Immortality in the Fourth Gospel," p. 294.
48. "Ferdinand Christian Baur," p. 156.
49. "Immortality in the Fourth Gospel," p. 288.
50. "Ferdinand Christian Baur," p. 156; "A Century of Change in New Testament Criticism," p. 622; "Immortality in the Fourth Gospel," p. 289; cf. *Jesus and Paul*, p. 250f.
51. *The Fourth Gospel in Research and Debate*, p. 288.
52. *Ibid.*, pp. 432, 434.
53. "The Sacrament of Footwashing," pp. 218, 220f.
54. "The Mythical Collapse of Historical Christianity," p. 732.
55. *The Founding of the Church*, p. 10; "Die Ergebnisse der Bibelkritik für Theologie und Praxis," p. 21; cf. *The Making of the New Testament*, pp. 54, 248.
56. *Jesus and Paul*, p. 37; *Christianity Old and New*, p. 10.
57. "The 'Defence' of the Fourth Gospel," p. 138.
58. *The Making of the New Testament*, p. 23.
59. *Ibid.*, p. 29.
60. "The 'Defence' of the Fourth Gospel," p. 138f.; cf. *He Opened To Us The Scriptures*, p. 98f.; *The Making of the New Testament*, p. 120; "The Gospel Paul 'Received'," p. 36.
61. *Jesus and Paul*, pp. 167-69; "The Resurrection in Byzantine Art," pp. 29, 31, 35; "The Resurrection in Primitive Tradition and Observance," p. 396; *The Making of the New Testament*, p. 17; "'Thankworthy' Goodness," p. 517f.; "The 'Defence' of the Fourth Gospel," p. 139.
62. *The Making of the New Testament*, pp. 108ff., 120; "The Doctrine of Faith in Hebrews, James, and Clement of Rome," *Journal of Biblical Literature*, XIX (1900), pp. 19, 21; "'Thankworthy' Goodness," p. 512; cf. *An Introduction to the New Testament*, p. 164.
63. *An Introduction to the New Testament*, pp. 142, 164f.; cf. "The Priesthood without Pedigree," *The Expository Times*, XIII (1902), p.

345f.; "Heb. 1:10-12 and the Septuagint Rendering of Ps. 102:23," *Zeitschrift für die neutestamentliche Wissenschaft*, III (1902), p. 284; "The Festival of Lives Given for the Nation in Jewish and Christian Faith," p. 273; "The Doctrine of Faith in Hebrews, James, and Clement of Rome," pp. 13f., 17, 19.

64. *Is Mark a Roman Gospel?* p. 104; *Jesus and Paul*, pp. 167-69.
65. *Jesus and Paul*, pp. 167-69.
66. "The Resurrection in Primitive Tradition and Observance," p. 402f.
67. *Jesus and Paul*, pp. 167-69.

CHAPTER SIX
BACON'S LIFE OF JESUS — AN OUTLINE

Bacon never achieved his intended goal — a life of Jesus. Yet, he considered the studies he had undertaken as indicating the direction such a life might take. The volumes to which he referred as furnishing a base for the projected "life" include *The Beginnings of Gospel Story*; *The Gospel of Mark*; *Studies in Matthew*; *The Fourth Gospel in Research and Debate*, and the posthumously published *The Gospel of the Hellenists*. Inferences may also be drawn from Bacon's *Jesus The Son of God*, of which he wrote that "should opportunity not be given for the contemplated Life this preliminary sketch will serve to indicate the lines along which it might be expected to develop."[1] Since, however, this volume is in essence a recapitulation of ideas contained in earlier studies, the latter together with the volumes cited above furnish most of the material for our sketch.

I: *The Galilean Phase*:

Fixing the nativity at about the year 6 B.C., Bacon described Jesus' Galilean ministry as constituting the first phase of his career.[2] According to Bacon, Jesus' work in Galilee was a continuation of John's and thus nothing more than the work of a prophet.[3] Nor, he added, did Jesus entertain the notion of founding a new religion.[4] Hence, whether in Galilee or in Jerusalem, Jesus was not conscious of any distinction between new and old in the fulfillment of his ministry.[5]

Bacon wrote that Matthew 11:2-19 and Luke 7:18-35 constituted Jesus' earliest utterance regarding the Baptist[6] whom he identified with the Elijah of Malachi 4:5, and whose task was to admit to Israel's inheritance those who had been wrongfully excluded and to exclude "men of violence" or those wrongfully admitted.[7] Jesus further identified the Baptist with "the Coming One" or "Reaper" about to execute Jahveh's long-deferred wrath.[8] Thus the fulfillment of both great and ancient personages was realized in the person of the Baptist.

On the other hand, Bacon continued, John identified Jesus with Elijah and the "Coming One" because he did not think beyond the "purification" of Israel.[9] As a consequence, Bacon argued, John's baptism was not a prophetic prolepsis of the Christian rite, but coincided with various pre-Christian baptizing sects of Judaism.[10] And, since Jesus took to himself the *work* of Elijah, and of himself said merely, "blessed is he who takes no offense at me," John's opinion had its corroboration in Jesus' own activity.

Stating that scrutiny of the records for evidence of Jesus' unknown personal history commended itself both from a religious and scientific point of view, Bacon believed the narratives of the baptism and temptation could be traced to a "positive autobiographic discourse from Jesus' own lips,"[11] delivered at Caesarea Philippi. He agreed with Beyschlag that Jesus *consciously* became Son of God at his baptism,[12] although he added that Jesus' Messianic call came by revelation and not by the "mere unaided reasonings of his own soul."[13] To this revelation may have been added a corresponding physical reaction resulting in a vision.[14] Translating the phrase in Mark 1:11 and parallels to read "my choice hath fallen upon thee" (whether now or in years past),[15] Bacon wrote that Jesus' own representation of the voice which sent him on his mission was simply "thou art my Son."[16] Interpreting Matthew's narrative as a later apologetic, Bacon stated it was not merely "to fulfill all righteousness" that Jesus was baptized. On the contrary, Jesus was not careful to draw distinction between his message and John's,[17] and thus was baptized along with the "men of violence." In examining the temptation story, Bacon cited Friedrich Spitta to the effect that the three solicitations of Satan "in some measure" corresponded to a real experience.[18] He nevertheless marked the symbolism in the narratives of both Matthew and Luke,[19] and described the event as a "conflict of soul," an encounter and conquest of unworthy ideas of Messiahship in Jesus' own mind.[20]

For Bacon the essence of Jesus' teaching lay in the doctrine of the restoration of the lost son to the father's house, a doctrine marking the culmination of the "Father-Theism" of the Old Testament.[21] At the same time, he described Jesus' idea of the Kingdom as new because he brought to it the conviction that it is a "filial relation" of trust and obedience, a "moral unity" with the Father, in contrast to the book-religion of precept and ceremonial.[22] This novelty, Bacon continued, corresponded to Jesus' own experience, for in the idea of the Kingdom Jesus found an ideal of life for himself, his country and all humanity.[23] The Kingdom was thus progressively to be attained by virtue of men's participation in a moral unity with the Father.[24] For this reason, he interpreted the $\dot{\epsilon}\nu\tau\dot{o}\varsigma\ \dot{\upsilon}\mu\hat{\omega}\nu$ of Luke 17:21 to mean "within you."[25] He then went on to write that in Jesus' teaching of the Kingdom we encounter that point at which the "gospel of" and the "gospel about" coincide — the gospel Paul proclaimed had for its content that One in whom absolute devotion to the Kingdom was incarnate.[26]

Contrasting apocalyptic representation with what he called the "gradual evolution of humanity under the law of love into a human-divine fellowship,"[27] Bacon first of all described apocalyptic eschatology as the

> fruit . . . of Jewish hatred and insane pride, born of the fanaticism of the Pharisee and Zealot in response to the fiendish oppression of an Antiochus Epiphanes and the long slavery of Rome.[28]

Bacon denied that the apocalyptic eschatology was typical of Jesus.[29] This did not mean, he added, that Jesus did not in some measure share the catastrophic eschatology of his time.[30] Still, Bacon contended, of all the types of Jewish literature which can be considered to have influenced Jesus' teaching, apocalyptic did not dominate because there was nothing in Jesus' "strong and steady career" which bespoke the visionary and ecstatic.[31] He wrote that since the utterances of Jesus subordinated the eschatological to the ethical, he was justified in referring to "the sane and well-poised mind of the plain mechanic of Nazareth,"[32] an epithet which e.g., F. C. Burkitt had found "reprehensible." Armed with the contention that evidence of Jesus' entertaining "fantastic dreams of apocalypse" had been reduced to nothing,[33] Bacon described the subsequent identification of Jesus with the Son of Man as originating "in the exalted and visionary expectations of a church on fire with momentary expectations of the end."[34] As a result, the Pauline transition to firmer ground than Jewish apocalypse had its basis in the essential teaching of Jesus.[35]

Bacon characterized this first phase of Jesus' ministry as a "protest" on behalf of the "little ones" against the "men of violence" who recognized as sons of the Kingdom only those submissive bearers of the yoke of the law as interpreted by them.[36] Jesus' "unquestionably historical" claim was that the wisdom of God, accessible to these "little ones" and hid from the wise and prudent, came by revelation.[37] The essence of this revelation, Bacon wrote, was the knowledge of God's righteousness as consisting in a "religious and mystical" morality footing upon the relation of the human to the divine. Such morality, Bacon contended, was not a better system of conduct, but the divinely given means of attaining a moral ideal already fixed.[38] In this connection, he described Jesus' word in Matthew 11:27 (Luke 10:22: "all things have been delivered to me by my Father") as the "nearest approach to the expression of a more than merely human self-consciousness,"[39] and as constituting Jesus' only alternative in face of the "men of violence."[40]

Thus, the form of a new law in which Jesus cast his teaching was a form only. His teaching was free of all restraint of tradition and convention,[41] for which reason departure from opinions gleaned from Jesus' particular age and environment was compatible with loyalty to him as a Teacher.[42] At any rate, legalism was totally foreign to Jesus' teaching.[43] His utterances concerning divorce (Mark 10:1-12) and his demurrer at the request to arbitrate (Luke 12:14), revealed his refusal to occupy the seat of magistrate in the imperfect conditions of the world.[44] Moreover, Jesus' view of the Sabbath was intended to make it a "delight," a day of the breaking of every yoke.[45] Hence, Bacon concluded, though the ideal of the genuine Pharisee and Jesus were the same, for the Pharisee God's will was revealed in the Torah, whereas for Jesus it was present in the heart.[46]

Bacon wrote that the immense reaction to Jesus' preaching was due not merely to the reawakening of prophetic authority, but also to certain startling accompaniments.[47] He stated that the miracles of healing, which "none today will be disposed to question as historical occurrences,"[48] first occasioned a prayer vigil (Mark 1:35-39), but were later welcomed by Jesus as a divine aid and seal upon his proclamation of forgiveness.[49] In this first phase, during which his consciousness was prophetic and not yet Messianic,[50] Jesus did not appeal to the miracles as proof of personal authority, but merely as evidences of the gracious presence and power of God.

At the conclusion of this first phase, Jesus' championing the "people of the land" and consequent invective against the "men of violence" brought him into irrepressible conflict with the scribes,[51] but it was a championing which gave him the right to be called Son of God and to defend that right with his life.[52] This phase, however, failed through unbelief, and Jesus' public work in Galilee was broken off.[53] He remained in hiding on the northern frontier until, after secretly rallying his adherents in Capernaum, he undertook with them the last emprise.[54]

II. *Phase Two — Caesarea Philippi*:

Bacon wrote that after Jesus had failed in Galilee, he consulted his few remaining followers at Caesarea Philippi regarding his career. The "campaign" had either to be abandoned or reopened on a larger, more perilous scale.[55] At Peter's suggestion, Jesus assumed the wholly new role and title of "the Christ."[56] With the assumption of this title, the movement of Jesus now took on a nationalistic character[57] which led him to his first public act in Judea, viz., the cleansing of the temple.[58] With this new phase, said Bacon, Jesus sounded the note of personal loyalty to himself in a manner thus far unknown.[59] Without this change, he maintained, the popular support given Jesus, his execution and the subsequent rallying to his banner would be historically unintelligible.[60]

Bacon went on to state that despite the congruence of the Messianic title with Jesus' purpose, he nevertheless stripped it of any theocratic connotations.[61] For example, though Davidic sonship was assumed to be an attribute of Messiah and Jesus' own Davidic descent was practically undisputed,[62] he refused to base any claim upon it. Indeed, his use of Psalm 100 (Mark 2:35-37 and parallels) challenged the notion of Davidic sonship as a matter of pedigree.[63] Throughout this entire second phase, Jesus and his immediate followers struggled to transcend the Jewish idea and to fix current expectations at the point of Jesus' "spiritual messianic claim"[64] to a kingship and priesthood which were his by divine appointment rather than by descent.[65] Jesus thus assumed his Messiahship in a purely ethico-religious sense, a sense which appeared figurative to his contemporaries but which Bacon contended was older than the monarchical.[66] For this reason, Jesus met Peter's suggestion of a coup d'etat at Caesarea Philippi with a rebuke of crushing severity.[67]

Bacon believed the Christology of the early community could be traced to Jesus' ethico-religious idea of Messiahship.[68] On the other hand, he described *belief* in such a Messiahship as deriving more from the ecstatic experiences of his adherents following his death than from words uttered during his lifetime.[69]

In Bacon's opinion, Jesus faced another alternative at Caesarea Philippi, that of the failure of his nationalistic movement.[70] Thus, on the occasion of Peter's confession the twelve first became acquainted with Jesus' anticipation of humiliation and death.[71] This is not to say, Bacon added, that Jesus left for Jerusalem to be crucified. Quite the contrary — the passion predictions were to be regarded as unhistorical.[72] The purpose of Jesus' journey was rather to fulfill his mission in spite of the menace of the cross[73] which was merely foreseen as an alternative.[74] In face of possible martyrdom, yet confident that God would not suffer his cause to fail, Jesus spoke of that transcendental being, the

"Son of Man," who was to advance John's work and vindicate his own cause.[75] This figure Bacon described as the "conventional" agent of God's vindication, and referred to Daniel 7:13 and Ethiopic Enoch as the principle sources of Jesus' doctrine.[76]

While Bacon refused to deny Jesus' use of the Son of Man title, insisting that Jesus had a Son of Man doctrine from the outset,[77] he did deny that the title was Jesus' favorite self-designation or was typical of him.[78] Consequently, he leaned toward the opinion that because Jesus did not aim at fulfilling the office of Son of Man in his own person, it was only after his death that references to this apocalyptic figure were applied to him.[79] Bacon buttressed his argument by again referring to Jesus' conception of sonship as ethical and religious. For Bacon this meant that the "sonship" or Messiahship to which Jesus laid claim was not his in any exclusive sense, but denoted adoption to sonship by virtue of the descent and indwelling of the Spirit.[80] Such a "religious" sonship, Bacon wrote, constituted the essence of the Messianic hope and the true prerogative of Israel.[81] Of this, he added, the recently discovered Odes of Solomon gave "irrefutable evidence."[82] Bacon continued that the *logion* in Matthew 11:27 = Luke 10:22 ("all things have been delivered to me by my Father, etc.") did not reflect a "superhuman consciousness," but rather the "capacity of normal unsullied human nature" for the divine wisdom.[83] Since, however, Jesus looked for a vindication of the "tribes of Jehovah," his simpler conception gave rise to the apocalyptic notion of apostolic times which assigned him the Son of Man title as if it had been his favorite.[84] Indeed, said Bacon, if Jesus did not actually claim to be the Christ, it is inconceivable that his words of promise could be later recalled as proving that his references to the coming Son of Man were mysterious self-designations.[85] Bacon also denied that Jesus identified himself with the Isaian Servant.[86] At the same time, he traced the concept as such to Jesus himself, since he made appeal to Isaiah's "glad tidings" as a parallel to his own ministry.[87] Thus, for the earliest community, the doctrine of the sacrificed Servant became what Bacon called the "bridge" between the crucified Jesus and the glorified figure of the Son of Man, agent of God's vindication.[88] To the extent Jesus was confident of that vindication and anticipated a martyr fate, to that extent he was responsible for the "merging of the two figures."[89]

As a result of his insistence upon the exclusively non-metaphysical, ethico-religious aspect of Jesus' sonship, Bacon asserted that the title which was truly characteristic of Jesus was that of "Son of God," a title with which the twelve first became acquainted at Caesarea Philippi.[90] Jesus claimed the title on behalf of those "little ones," and since in his life and death he had incarnated the principle of absolute devotion to the Kingdom, he could without incongruity be declared to be the "Son of God with power by the resurrection from the dead."[91]

III: Phase Three — Judea, Death and Resurrection:

Cherishing national aspirations so as to rally the scattered children of God and conscious that the scribes had remained masters of the field after he had attacked the usurpations of the synogogue, Jesus now resolved to advance to the central citadel and challenge the primal usurpation in the temple itself.[92] His first public act in Judea was thus the cleansing of the temple. Bacon described this coup d'etat as the climax of Jesus' career, planned with careful deliberation, and symbolizing the significance of his national mission. Jesus staked all on that event.[93] As things turned out, his control of the sanctuary was short-lived.[94] According to Bacon, this new failure marked still another phase in Jesus' ministry — that of dedicated priest and intercessor before God. Deliberately dedicating himself to a fate like John's, Jesus now resolved to give his life as an atonement-offering.[95] This was not an innovation, wrote Bacon, but it was a new teaching never heard in Galilee.[96] Nor, Bacon hastened to add, was it a dedication which violated the principle of individual accountability.[97] For this reason, Jesus did not intend to introduce a doctrine of "substitutionary atonement" at the Last Supper.[98] His death

would be for "the many," that the new Israel might receive
God's favor.[99] This concept of forgiveness for Christ's
sake — fundamental to the idea of Christ as Suffering
Servant, and with its deposit only in the First Epistle of
Peter — was connected with Peter's "turning again" and
constituted Peter's call to the apostleship of the circumcision
a fit prelude to the experience and gospel of Paul.[100]

From the outset, Bacon wrote, Jesus' crucifixion was the
result of a secret plot.[101] The hierarchy could adduce only
one item in evidence against him, the fact that he had lifted
his hand against the priests' control of the temple.[102] For this
reason, Bacon asserted, Jesus' detention by the Sanhedrin
involved an illegal seizure.[103] Judas' report merely furnished
the conspirators a pretext they had thus far sought in vain.[104]
In a discussion of the Bethany anointing (John 12:1-8)
against the background of the secret coronation of Jehu in II
Kings 9, Bacon concluded that what Judas actually betrayed
was that while Jesus sat at table in the house of Simon the
leper, he had been formally, though secretly, anointed "King
of the Jews."[105]

As a result of Judas' act, wrote Bacon, but also in
consequence of Jesus' refusal to deny national aspirations
and designs, he was executed by Roman authority as a
messianic agitator and disturber of the peace.[106] He died, as
the Fourth Gospel records, on the fourteenth of Nisan, when
the lambs were slain in preparation for Passover.[107]
Rejecting the "Lukan" dating of the crucifixion between the
years A.D. 28 and 29, Bacon affirmed that the most probable
date for the Passion was A. D. 33 or 34, or, following John,
forty to forty-nine years from the nativity.[108]

Bacon fixed the date of the resurrection on Sunday,
Nisan 16th, when the first-fruits or $\dot{\alpha}\pi\alpha\rho\chi\dot{\eta}$ were offered in
the temple,[109] and referred to the resurrection appearances as
"psychological."[110] Jesus thus was seen "in vision" by those
who had companied with him.[111] On occasion Bacon
appeared to assume the experiences of the risen Lord were
self-induced,[112] and yet referred to the "apotheosis" as a
"revelation," as "received," or spoke of a "direct spiritual
intervention from the unseen world."[113] But he was more

fascinated by the question of the "why" of the disciples' experience, whatever its nature. Referring to Jewish distaste for the notion of mere immortality,[114] Bacon described the *national* hope as rooted in the idea of a special resurrection for heroes and martyrs who had given their lives for the redemption of God's people.[115] Jesus' farewell discourse and the Last Supper constituted a "preparatory nucleus" for the resurrection experience, since both events fell within the context of death on behalf of the other.[116] The Golgotha event thus introduced a new element into the "Christian doctrine of immortality."[117] Further, Bacon pointed to the "character and career of Jesus the Nazarene" as yielding an explanation for the Christian community's apotheosis-resurrection doctrine.[118] Jesus, he said, could not have been manifested as Son of God with power if he had not first been known as one whose "moral qualities" entitled him to such enthronement.[119] Indeed, the revelation made clear to Peter and the Twelve that he had been the Son of God as he had taught others to be.[120] Nothing else than a doctrine of apotheosis, then, could express the significance of the career which his followers had witnessed.[121]

Bacon located the resurrection in Peter's "turning again" (Luke 22:31-32), and described it as originating in a recollection of the words of Jesus who had promised to make his disciples' cause his own; in the "memory" of Peter's personal and intimate relation with Jesus, or in a direct "spiritual" intervention.[122] In any event, that "turning again" spelled the transition from Jewish Messianism to Christian Christology in its peculiarly ethico-religious form.[123] In this sense, too, Jesus' Christology had lain at the root of the reawakening.[124]

For Bacon, the next step was the rallying of the Twelve, for which Peter's experience furnished the motive and occasion — the disciples' inward vision was quickened to see what Peter had already seen.[125] Bacon concluded that though the experience of the risen Christ was a "problem of religious psychology, and not of history," that experience alone accounts for the preservation of Jesus' story and furnishes explanation to the origins of Christianity.[126] In

other words, this essentially Petrine experience or "gospel
about Jesus" yielded Paul the gospel he "received" and set in
motion that train of events of which the New Testament
Gospels and Epistles are the reflection. "Our religion," wrote
Bacon, "began with the manifestation of the Son of God."[127]

---

1. *Studies in Matthew*, p. 518.
2. "Notes on Gospel Chronology," pp. 130, 148; *Jesus and Paul*, pp. 38, 40.
3. "Jesus Christ," p. 164f.; *Jesus and Paul*, pp. 38, 40; "The 'Coming One' of John the Baptist," *The Expositor*, X (1904), pp. 16ff.
4. *The Founding of the Church*, p. 4.
5. "New and Old in Jesus' Relation to John," p. 80.
6. "The Baptism of John — Where Was It?" p. 40.
7. *Jesus The Son Of God or Primitive Christology*, p. 26f.; *He Opened To Us The Scriptures*, p. 76; "New and Old in Jesus' Relation to John," p. 78.
8. "The 'Coming One' of John the Baptist," pp. 3, 11, 13f.
9. *Ibid.*, p. 16.
10. "Is Baptism Syncretistic?" p. 160.
11. "The Autobiography of Jesus," *The American Journal of Theology*, II (1898), pp. 527, 530, 538; "The Temptation of Jesus: His Conception of Messiahship," *The Biblical World*, XV (1900), p. 19; "Jesus' Voice from Heaven," p. 472; cf. *The Beginnings of Gospel Story*, p. 124.
12. "The Autobiography of Jesus," p. 530f., n. 8; 543f., n. 27; *The Story of Jesus and the Beginnings of the Church*, p. 324.
13. "The Autobiography of Jesus," pp. 543f., 551.
14. *Ibid.*, p. 552.
15. "Notes on New Testament Passages," *Journal of Biblical Literature* n XVI (1897), p. 138.
16. For Bacon, the Isaian ending was merely an epexegetical addition, no doubt derived from the transfiguration story. It was a revelation in "vision" to Peter and those with him of the Isaian doctrine of the Servant of God. Cf. "Jesus' Voice from Heaven," p. 471f.
17. Though difference there was — to John the Kingdom was imminent, to Jesus it was immanent, cf. "New and Old in Jesus' Relation to John," pp. 68, 70.
18. "Spitta's *Urchristliche Literatur*," *The American Journal of Theology*, XIII (1909), p. 127.
19. "The Autobiography of Jesus," p. 538.
20. *Ibid.*, p. 555.
21. "The Temptation of Jesus: His Conception of the Messiahship," p. 22; "Die Ergebnisse der Bibelkritik für Theologie und Praxis," p. 21.

22. "Jesus' Voice from Heaven," p. 471; *Studies in Matthew*, p. 346; *The Founding of the Church*, p. 5.

23. "Right and Wrong Use of the Bible," p. 394; *Commentary on The Epistle of Paul to the Galatians*, p. 117. Bacon wrote that the vital feature in e.g., the narrative of the Syro-Phoenician woman was her reply which Jesus conceived as enlarging his own point of view, cf. *The Beginnings of Gospel Story*, p. 90.

24. "Die Ergebnisse der Bibelkritik für Theologie und Praxis," p. 21.

25. "The End of the World," *The Old and New Testament Student*, XIII (1891), p. 229.

26. "Royce's Interpretation of Christianity," p. 333f.

27. "The End of the World," p. 229.

28. *Ibid.*, p. 233.

29. *The Apostolic Message*, p. 218; "Immortality in the Synoptic Gospels," p. 202.

30. "Ultimate Problems of Biblical Science," p. 6.

31. *Jesus The Son of God*, p. 43.

32. *Is Mark a Roman Gospel?* p. 88f.; "Royce's Interpretation of Christianity," p. 330; *The Apostolic Message*, p. 219.

33. "Jesus as Son of Man," *The Harvard Theological Review*, III (1910), p. 338.

34. *Ibid.*, p. 340.

35. *The Apostolic Message*, p. 220.

36. "Jesus Christ," p. 165; "Mystery," *A Dictionary of Christ and the Gospels*, II, 214; *Jesus The Son Of God or Primitive Christology*, p. 27f.

37. "Mystery," p. 214.

38. "Why Callest Thou Me Good?" p. 337f.

39. "Gospel Criticism and Christian Origins," p. 623.

40. *Jesus The Son Of God or Primitive Christology*, p. 28f.

41. "Ultimate Problems of Biblical Science," p. 7.

42. *Ibid.*, pp. 4, 7.

43. *The Sermon on the Mount*, p. 114.

44. *Ibid.*, p. 177f.

45. "The Sabbath, Jewish and Christian," *Yale Divinity Quarterly*, IX (1913), p. 121.

46. "The Relations of New Testament Science to Kindred Sciences," p. 583f. When the Jewish scholar Claude Montefiore described Jesus' moral and religious teaching as the best the Rabbis taught and attempted to coordinate Jesus' life and teaching with Judaism, Bacon queried, "why was not Jesus Himself both scribe and Pharisee?" and admitted he much preferred the studies of Moritz Friedländer, who had described Judaism's legalistic development as a narrowing reaction and had written of Jesus as a truer successor of the prophets and the Chasidim; cf. "Jewish Interpretations of the New Testament," pp. 169, 172, 174.

47. "Jesus Christ," p. 165.

48. "The Success and Failure of Liberalism," p. 99f.
49. "Jesus Christ," p. 165; *Studies in Matthew*, p. 392; cf. "The 'Son of Man' in the Usage of Jesus," p. 164.
50. *Studies in Matthew*, p. 393.
51. "Jesus Christ," p. 165; *Jesus The Son Of God or Primitive Christology*, p. 27.
52. *Ibid.*
53. *Jesus and Paul*, pp. 38, 40, 42.
54. "Jesus Christ," p. 166.
55. *Ibid.*
56. *The Beginnings of Gospel Story*, p. 107f.; *The Founding of the Church*, p. 11f.; cf. "What Did Judas Betray?" *The Hibbert Journal*, XIX (1921), p. 492f.
57. "The 'Son of Man' in the Usage of Jesus," p. 147; *Jesus and Paul*, p. 45.
58. *The Story of Jesus and the Beginnings of the Church*, p. 232.
59. *The Beginnings of Gospel Story*, p. 119; "The 'Son of Man' in the Usage of Jesus," p. 152.
60. Cf. *The Story of Jesus and the Beginnings of the Church*, pp. 217, 223f.
61. *The Beginnings of Gospel Story*, p. 107.
62. "Genealogy of Jesus Christ," p. 138.
63. "Gospel Types in Primitive Tradition," p. 887; "The Priesthood without Pedigree," p. 348.
64. "Genealogy of Jesus Christ," p. 141.
65. "Gospel Types in Primitive Tradition," p. 887; "The Priesthood without Pedigree," p. 348.
66. *The Founding of the Church*, p. 11f.; *Jesus The Son Of God or Primitive Christology*, p. 100; cf. "Jesus as Lord," p. 204; "The Relations of New Testament Science to Kindred Sciences," p. 583.
67. "Jesus Christ," p. 166.
68. *Jesus The Son Of God or Primitive Christology*, p. 100.
69. "Jesus as Son of Man," p. 327.
70. "The 'Son of Man' in the Usage of Jesus," p. 147.
71. "The Transfiguration Story," p. 239.
72. *The Story of Jesus and the Beginnings of the Church*, p. 217.
73. *The Apostolic Message*, p. 234.
74. *The Beginnings of Gospel Story*, p. 109; "The 'Son of Man' in the Usage of Jesus," p. 147; "The Transfiguration Story," p. 239.
75. *The Founding of the Church*, p. 50; "The 'Son of Man' in the Usage of Jesus," pp. 147, 176f.; *The Beginnings of Gospel Story*, p. 109. Bacon challenged that school of criticism which was so enamored of Mark's portrait of the prophet with supernatural foresight that it conceived Jesus as provoking the fate he suffered in Jerusalem so as to achieve the glory of the Son of Man, cf. *The Story of Jesus and the Beginnings of the Church*, p. 224.
76. *The Beginnings of Gospel Story*, p. 108f.; *The Apostolic Message*, p. 222; *Studies in Matthew*, pp. 421, 431.

77. "The Relations of New Testament Science to Kindred Sciences," p. 581; "The 'Son of Man' in the Usage of Jesus," p. 145; "Jesus as Son of Man," p. 330. Cf. "Primitive Christianity," pp. 757, 760, in which Bacon described Pfleiderer's denial that Jesus ever applied the title to himself as stretching a justifiable principle of criticism to an unjustifiable extreme.

78. *The Beginnings of Gospel Story*, p. 108; *The Apostolic Message*, p. 218f.; *Jesus The Son Of God or Primitive Christology*, p. 20.

79. *The Beginnings of Gospel Story*, p. 108f.; *The Founding of the Church*, p. 50; *The Apostolic Message*, p. 222; cf. *Studies in Matthew*, pp. 421, 426; "The 'Son of Man' in the Usage of Jesus," pp. 145, 158, 182; "Jesus as Son of Man," p. 330.

80. *Jesus The Son Of God or Primitive Christology*, pp. 14, 27ff. Bacon earlier pointed to Jesus' disclaimer of divine attributes as recorded by Mark, cf. "Why Callest Thou Me Good?" p. 345f.

81. *Jesus The Son Of God or Primitive Christology*, p. 23.

82. "Jesus as Lord," p. 204. Stimulated by J. Rendel Harris' discovery of the Odes, Bacon, despite his admittedly inadequate knowledge of Syriac, undertook an independent investigation. His conclusion was that the author was not dependent on Christian ideas, but rather on Deutero-Isaiah, the Wisdom of Solomon and the Stoic doctrine of the Logos. Though he admitted the difficulty of separating Christian interpolations from the original substance, he nevertheless laid down the general rule that the strongest evidence of textual corruption lay where the Christian element was most pronounced, and concluded that the earliest date to which the interpolated material could be traced was the beginning of the fourth century. Bacon contended that such concepts as the Odes' doctrine of immortality, derived from the concept of the Servant in Deutero-Isaiah, proved that the transition from Judaism and kindred cults to Christianity was far less abrupt than scholars had fancied. Cf. "The Odes of the Lord's Rest," *The Expositor*, I (1911), pp. 194f., n.2, 203; "Songs of the Lord's Beloved," *The Expositor*, I (1911), pp. 323, 325, 329, 331, 334; "The Odes of Solomon: Christian Elements," *The Expositor*, II (1911), p. 256; "Further Light on the Odes of Solomon," *The Expositor*, IV (1912), p. 462.

83. "Gospel Criticism and Christian Origins," p. 623f.; cf. *Jesus The Son Of God or Primitive Christology*, p. 1. Early in his career, Bacon spoke of Jesus' "choice" of the Son of Man title because it expressed his utter dependence upon God, cf. "Why Callest Thou Me Good?" p. 346.

84. *Studies in Matthew*, pp. 421, 426; "The 'Son of Man' in the Usage of Jesus," pp. 177, 181; *The Beginnings of Gospel Story*, p. 108.

85. "The 'Son of Man' in the Usage of Jesus," p. 181f.

86. *The Apostolic Message*, p. 222. Earlier, Bacon had merely insisted that the Isaiah figure did not dominate Jesus' thought, cf. "Jesus' Voice from Heaven," p. 470.

87. *He Opened To Us The Scriptures,* p. 76; "The 'Son of Man' in the Usage of Jesus," p. 179f.; "The Gospel Paul 'Received'," p. 39.
88. "The 'Son of Man' in the Usage of Jesus," pp. 147, 149.
89. *Ibid.*
90. *Jesus The Son Of God or Primitive Christology,* pp. 20, 28f.; "Jesus as Lord," p. 204; *Jesus The Son of God,* p. 85; "The Transfiguration Story," p. 239.
91. "Royce's Interpretation of Christianity," p. 334.
92. *The Beginnings of Gospel Story,* p. 161.
93. "Non-Resistance: Christian or Pagan?" *Religion and the War* (New Haven: Yale University Press, 1918), p. 62f.; "Christus Militans," *The Hibbert Journal,* XVI (1918), p. 549f.; *Jesus and Paul,* p. 30. Did Bacon construe Peter's suggestion of a coup at Caesarea Philippi in terms of a capture of Jerusalem as a whole and thus distinct from the temple cleansing, or did he conceive the cleansing as such as expressive of Jesus' change of plan?
94. "Jesus Christ," p. 166f.; *Jesus and Paul,* p. 50.
95. "New and Old in Jesus' Relation to John," p. 78; *Jesus The Son of God,* p. 60, n. 7; *Jesus and Paul,* pp. 45, 50.
96. *Jesus and Paul,* p. 50.
97. *The Apostolic Message,* p. 349, cf. 388.
98. *Ibid.,* p. 340.
99. *Ibid.,* p. 349.
100. *The Story of Jesus and the Beginnings of the Church,* p. 319.
101. "What Did Judas Betray?" p. 486; *The Gospel of Mark,* p. 171.
102. *The Beginnings of Gospel Story,* p. 211.
103. Bacon clearly preferred the Fourth Gospel's representation of the gathering of the Sanhedrin, cf. *The Story of Jesus and the Beginnings of the Church,* p. 246f., and "Jesus Christ," p. 167.
104. "What Did Judas Betray?" p. 492.
105. *Ibid.,* p. 490, 492f.
106. *Ibid.,* p. 486; "Jesus Christ,"p. 167; "Christus Militans," p. 548; *The Story of Jesus and the Beginnings of the Church,* p. 223f.
107. *An Introduction to the New Testament,* p. 267; "The Resurrection in Primitive Tradition and Observance," p. 400.
108. "Lukan versus Johannine Chronology," pp. 209, 212; "Notes on Gospel Chronology," pp. 130, 148.
109. *An Introduction to the New Testament,* p. 267.
110. "Royce's Interpretation of Christianity," p. 332.
111. "Jesus Christ," p. 162; *Christianity Old and New,* p. 70f.; "The Return to Theology," p. 119.
112. "Immortality in the Synoptic Gospels," p. 221; "The Mythical Collapse of Historical Christianity," p. 743; *Christianity Old and New,* p. 134f.; "Jesus Christ," p. 167; "Jesus as Lord," pp. 213, 215, 228.
113. *The Founding of the Church,* p. 61; *Christianity Old and New,* p. 135f.; "Jesus Christ," p. 167.

114. "Immortality in the Synoptic Gospels," p. 212.

115. *Ibid.*, p. 220.

116. *Ibid.*, p. 214.

117. *Ibid.*, p. 221.

118. "Royce's Interpretation of Christianity," p. 332.

119. *Christianity Old and New*, p. 135; "The Mythical Collapse of Historical Christianity," p. 743.

120. *The Founding of the Church*, p. 61.

121. "The Mythical Collapse of Historical Christianity," p. 743.

122. *Jesus and Paul*, p. 113; *Jesus The Son Of God or Primitive Christology*, p. 100; "Jesus Christ," p. 167.

123. *Jesus The Son Of God or Primitive Christology*, p. 100f.

124. *Ibid.*, p. 98. Early in life, Bacon had suggested that the story of Christ's revelation to Peter originally referred to the post-resurrection appearance narrated in Luke 24:34 and I Corinthians 15:5. In process of time, this narrative was then transferred to Caesarea Philippi, eliminating elements offensive to Peter's adherents and including eschatological doctrines which the church was ultimately driven to incorporate from Paul's gospel. Cf. "The Transfiguration Story," p. 264f.

125. *The Story of Jesus and the Beginnings of the Church*, p. 292; *Jesus and Paul*, p. 113.

126. "Jesus Christ," p. 162.

127. *Christianity Old and New*, p. 70f.

CHAPTER SEVEN:
EVALUATION

I: *Introduction*:

The third edition of *Die Religion in Geschichte und Gegenwart* omits all mention of Bacon, and a recent Roman Catholic work on the Fourth Gospel identifies him as an Anglican.[1] Such omissions and mislocations, however, are an exception to the universal attention paid the Yale scholar during and following his years of activity. His work elicited praise from scholars here and abroad, among them H. J. Cadbury, Carl Clemen, B. S. Easton, E. C. Hoskyns, W. F. Howard, Adolf Jülicher, Arnold Meyer, James Moffatt and Vincent Taylor.[2]

Obviously, the author of more than two hundred and sixty articles, monographs, essays and volumes was not free from attack. One critic wrote that it was not easy for Bacon to write in clear, popular fashion, and another that it was difficult in Bacon's work to see the wood for the trees.[3] More than once, he was accused of plunging into matters *in medias res*, of assuming results without indicating how they were achieved.[4] But Bacon was not merely faulted for lack of clarity. Many thought him a trifle too clever and his ideas too contrived to gain acceptance. Ernest Findlay Scott wrote of Bacon's almost fiendish delight in the intricate and bizarre that

> a feeling of something like pity comes over the reader as he watches each poor phrase or incident laid on the rack and compelled to yield its reluctant confession. He doubts whether he can rely on evidence wrung out by torture. He finds himself wondering if there is not some more obvious answer to the riddles which are solved so ingeniously.[5]

No doubt, Bacon liberally employed the tool of conjecture. His notion that Jesus related his "autobiography" at Caesarea Philippi, that Judas betrayed his secret anointing and that "S" constituted a complete Gospel appear to offend against his own rule, viz., that conjecture is admissible "under appropriate safeguards sufficient to exclude unwarranted inferences and subjective fancy." Reference to such imaginings, however, as "impugning" the historicity of the narratives in question,[6] is scarcely to the point. Still and all, Bacon retained a certain notoriety for his "wild constructions."[7] For others, that very appetite for the intricate and theoretical held a certain charm.[8]

Alongside Bacon's frequent lack of clarity and his preoccupation with hypotheses few were minded to allow,[9] there was a sanguine, aggressive side to the man which drew friends and foes. Moffatt referred to his "dashing, slashing criticism of traditions ancient and modern," which made the study of his critical work enjoyable and profitable,[10] and W. F. Howard judged Bacon's "scornfully polemical work," *The Fourth Gospel in Research and Debate*, as his weightiest contribution to the critical discussion.[11] Some, of course, were offended by Bacon's perennial lust for combat.[12] Principal James Drummond appeared to have suffered most from Bacon's aggressiveness. Prepared for tranquil retirement, the aging scholar awoke to find himself pilloried in Bacon's volume on the Fourth Gospel, and spent the better part of an article in lachrymose defense.[13]

II: *Nullius Addicus!*

The exhausting and often frustrating examination of everything Benjamin Wisner Bacon ever wrote yields at least one solid impression — the man's persistent urge to get free, free of an authoritarianism resident in the scribal tradition of the "Princeton Theology" at home or of Ritschlianism abroad. For him, an interpretation of faith as assent to dogmas buttressed by facts extracted from Scripture, or an understanding of religion as rooted in the moral consciousness, spelled legalism pure and simple.[14] Those mottoes he was forever citing — "follow the truth if it takes you over Niagara" (a mot attributed to Nathaniel Taylor);

"the truth without fear or favor;" *nullius addictus jurare in verba magistri* (paraphrase of a line from Horace) — show that urge in him. And Bacon's heroes — Jonathan Edwards, the Dwights, Nathaniel Taylor and Theodore Thornton Munger, advocate of the "inalienable free agency of the soul"[15] — at least according to his own lights, stood for nothing if not for such freedom as he hankered after. This freedom, Bacon believed, attained concrete expression in that wedding of church and school achieved by the Pilgrim community and of which Yale was the shining example.[16] It is striking that a man bent on freedom from authoritarianism should have praised what contemporary analysis blames for a majority of the nation's current ills — Puritanism. Obviously, Bacon saw more in it than witch-hunting, Arthur Dimmesdale and the stocks.

And, since the bogey was scribalism, Bacon believed the route to freedom lay with biblical criticism. Freedom had to be won by means of a critical attack on a religion which had substituted the authority of the Book for that of the Spirit. It was that belief that led him to pore over the writings of Ladd while a fledgling at Lyme, to master Dutch and devour the volumes of W. Robertson Smith, the "martyr" of Aberdeen. It lay at the root of his eagerness to join Harper's circle and break a lance with Princeton's William Henry Green and gives explanation for his hunting out those diverse types while on leave from Yale in the summer of '97. Later, Bacon would learn to differentiate between the Beyschlags, Wellhausens and Weisses, but they all had one thing in common — freedom from the authority of the Book. Not one was a biblicist. Theodor Zahn's confidence in the reliability of ecclesiastical tradition rendered him too narrow and straight-laced for the young instructor. Not even Adolf Schlatter had appeal for the six-foot Eli who revelled at the Congress of Modernists in 1910, and whose encounter with Albert Loisy at Pontigny remained one of the signal experiences of his life.

To what extent this passion for freedom affected the whole of Bacon's theology may be open to debate, but it can be demonstrated that whatever smacked of the legal got short shrift with him. Bacon cast Jesus in the role of prophet versus scribe. He regarded the Gospels of Matthew and Luke as legalistic and insofar unhistorical and viewed the "gospel about Jesus" as antidote to the legal and juridical construed as past authority establishable by critical means.[17] The characterization of Bacon as a "liberal" or "modernist,"[18] and the attempt to identify him with Wilhelm Herrmann, C. Emmet, E. Abbot, H. B. Sharman, Percy Gardner, E. C. Denwich and others of like caste[19] was patently an error, though there were, of course, similarities.[20] But it was an error because it failed to appreciate that strain in Bacon which refused to establish faith on grounds amenable to technical, historical research.

In a subsequent period, the very criticisms levelled at Bacon, to the effect that he relegated the historical Jesus to the rank of a non-Christian, of a mere imitator,[21] or that he demoted him to a position below that of a Rabbi,[22] would be aimed at another great biblical critic of whose method and theological disposition his own was so reminiscent — Rudolf Bultmann. Passion for Paul and the "gospel about Jesus" take their explanation from that urge to get free, not merely from the trammels of a dogmatic which had overlain the Jesus tradition, but also from a legalism into which Continental liberalism had fallen by its attempt to make whatever it could uncover of the historical Jesus a foundation for belief. Bacon's apparent disinterest in the historical Jesus or his suggestion that in the course of the evolutionary chain of events one greater than Jesus might appear, may all be read from out of the context of his passion to free faith from dependence. But it was the method by which Bacon advanced to his work and which he believed would guarantee the freedom he was after which made him a founder.

III: *Aetiological Method and Modern Criticism:*

Careful readers will not miss the similarity between Bacon's "aetiological method," its corollary, "the method of pragmatic values," and form-critical research on the Continent. Bacon's colleague, Frank Porter, marked the similarity at once. Noting that the cliché "higher criticism" had fallen on bad times since Martin Dibelius had introduced the term *Formgeschichte* in 1919, Porter stated that it was precisely what passed for form criticism in Germany, or, "social environment research" at the University of Chicago, which Bacon had undertaken to add to the traditional source-criticism of the New Testament.[23] After comparing Dibelius' definition of *Formgeschichte* with statements drawn from Bacon's preface to *The Beginnings of Gospel Story* written in 1909, Porter concluded that a comparison of the two not only explained the fundamental purpose and method of the higher criticism as Bacon viewed it, but also suggested the originality and significance of his work as anticipatory of contemporary research. Ernest W. Burch, in a review of Bacon's *Jesus the Son of God*, commented that this little volume would probably stand as a contribution to the American species of form criticism, if such a type could be said to exist,[24] and Cadbury wrote of *Beginnings* that it remained the best illustration of the application of New Testament analysis on the basis of hypothetical sources and theological motifs.[25]

Bacon himself was not unaware that *Beginnings* had been declared to anticipate form-critical method,[26] nor was he ignorant of form-critical study in Europe. He made reference to Karl Ludwig Schmidt's *Der Rahmen der Geschichte Jesu* (1919) as giving the most systematic presentation of precisely the same line of study as concerned him in *The Gospel of Mark*.[27] He cited Bultmann's *Die Geschichte der synoptischen Tradition* as summing up the results of form criticism,[28] and spoke of Karl Kundsin's *Topologische Überlieferungsstoffe im Johannesevangelium* (1925) as having taught him to interpret geographical data in the Fourth Gospel in theological fashion.[29]

For Bacon, then, higher criticism as applied to the New Testament documents suggested more than a mere source analysis. It rather embraced the study of motives and causes, the "recovery of persons" — everything which later came to be associated with the school of form criticism.

If Bultmann's early studies aroused only modest debate among his contemporaries — the deluge of criticism being reserved for his later years — conservative reaction to Bacon's methods showed itself early. One English publication described him as a "critic of the destructive order," an unsafe guide ludicrously applying to the biblical narratives tests impossible to apply to Thucydides or Tacitus.[30] J. Gresham Machen of Princeton wrote that Bacon's attempt to demonstrate modern liberalism's affinity with Jesus and Paul had resulted in a "boundless modernizing," and characterized *He Opened To Us The Scriptures* as an attempt to show that a man may reject the truth of the Bible and still use it as Paul and Jesus did.[31] An Oxford scholar noted that Bacon dealt drastically with the Gospel accounts, and another from Edinburgh faulted him for reducing the Church's beginnings to the psychology of a movement which, beginning with data interpreted in non-supernatural fashion, culminated in a religion permeated with the supernatural, and concluded that he should not like to call Bacon a Unitarian, though he was certainly not a Trinitarian.[32] E. S. Buchanan attacked Bacon for treating the entire primitive Christian community as a gang of charlatans and forgers.[33] The attacks were inevitable. A man whose great-aunt had written that Shakespeare's plays were composed by a syndicate,[34] whose grandfather, Leonard, had championed Henry Ward Beecher and welcomed the biblical criticism of Timothy Colenso and W. Robertson Smith, and whose father had translated Pere Hyacinthe in the interest of the Old Catholic movement, could scarcely avoid the conservative's references to his origins as furnishing an explanation for his temerity.[35] One philosopher reasoned that such modification of Christianity as Bacon's work reflected might so alter its nature as to render it only a shadow of its former self, and implied that Bacon's avoidance of the supernatural served to reinforce the suspicion that Protestantism logically led to atheism.[36]

Readers were specifically cautioned against Bacon's indifference to the historical Jesus. "What we are really

invited to do," wrote *The Athenaeum's* anonymous author,
"is to engage in the consideration of the teaching of certain
Churches regarding Christ, and of course, we are not to
expect to find the historical Jesus."[37] J. M. Thompson
characterized *Christianity Old and New* as an abortive
attempt to synthesize nineteenth century liberalism's
recovery of the "religion of" with twentieth century
idealism's accent on the "religion about Jesus."[38] A reviewer
in the *London Times* referred to Bacon's pessimism
concerning the Gospel portrait of Jesus and cozily added
that since much in Bacon was hypothetical, many of his
readers would dissent on "crucial points."[39] Even Bacon's
long-time friend, Frank Porter, charged that his colleague
had characterized Jesus without using a single authentic
utterance — an excess of criticism, said Porter, for which
there was no warrant.[40]

Criticism of Bacon naturally directed itself against his
interpretation of the Gospels as adaptations to the needs and
beliefs of the post-apostolic age, and in particular against his
interpretation of the two Gospels to which he devoted the
major part of his energy — Mark and John. Machen,
exercised by Bacon's "liberal" views, roundly denied that the
earliest Gospel's representation was the product of late
development, and as if having proved the same therewith
triumphantly announced that "all the tendency-criticism of
Bacon falls to the ground."[41] In a review of *The Gospel of
Mark*, *The Expository Times* stated that a knowledge of the
nature and date of Mark was poor compensation for the loss
of the Gospel itself, and giving special attention to Bacon's
discovery of Midrashic elements in the narrative of Jesus'
baptism denied that an account so historically and
psychologically probable required such explanation.[42] The
ever critical Buchanan reckoned that Bacon preferred Mark
among the Synoptists, though that Gospel had been reduced
to unreliability by virtue of its alleged composite, ill-digested
Christology and massive supernaturalism.[43] Lagrange, a
permanent and pertinacious foe, declared that Bacon's work
on Mark represented an intermediate stage between the
reaction of von Harnack and the "unbridled audacities" of
the extremists.[44]

"The Fourth Gospel," wrote *The Athenaeum's* reviewer, "is to [Bacon] nothing more than the story of Christ as told by the Church of the second century for its generation," and in light of Bacon's reference to his volume on John as semi-popular queried:

> Is the admission of semi-popularity an excuse for the sentence: 'The more unreformed critic might prefer not to be required to take the sacred writer's professed devotion to truth and loyalty to the concrete facts of history in a Pickwickian sense'?[45]

Commenting on *The Fourth Gospel in Research and Debate*, Arnold Meyer stated that Bacon's separation of chapter 21; his references to "R"; his deletion of 19:35, the Cana-miracle and temple-cleansing as well as his shifting of the Nicodemus pericope[46] rendered everything doubtful, and that by suddenly breaking off his argument[47]

> he simply lets us stand at the road leading beyond, not knowing how far we still must travel, then congratulates the critics who have brought such a pretty result to light, so that for sheer demoralization and mutilation we no longer know how to go in or out.[48]

Attacking Bacon for confusing the Gospel's topographical details,[49] Lagrange charged that his description of the Fourth Gospel as a defense of Paulinism — according to Bacon, an historical error though a spiritual verity — was unintelligible, a "subtle, clever, paradoxical psychology" fathered by Loisy.[50] Hoskyns wrote that Bacon's work on John served merely to reinforce the contention tha. Paul Wernle's idea of the Fourth Gospel as a mere echo of Paul was becoming widespread.[51]

In his thumbnail history of the interpretation of the New Testament between the years 1900 and 1950, Archibald Hunter summarized Bacon's view of the Fourth Gospel as a treatise whose primary aim is not fact but truth, whose discourses are theology not history, whose amalgam of anecdote, dialogue and allegory is only an application of Paul's doctrine of the Incarnation in terms of the Stoic Logos-theory, and concluded that Bacon was a "brilliant and ingenious man" whose speculations had won little acceptance.[52] Principal James Denney, however, delivered the majority "orthodox" opinion when he wrote of *The Fourth Gospel*:

> The book taken altogether is both brilliant and wrong-headed: it would be a fine book to go through, a chapter at a time, in a seminary; but the idea of offering it to the lay public to initiate it into the debate is astounding. The only conclusion to which the lay mind could come — and it would come to it promptly and decidedly — would be that, if 'John' is anything like what Bacon thinks, the less we trouble ourselves about him the better.[53]

Among Bacon's contemporaries, only Porter suggested he had not been radical enough, and noted in his friend a curious combination of conservatism and critical tendency:

> Not infrequently [Bacon] gives judgments of value and of ultimate truth, and usually these judgments are on the side of traditional Christian teaching and belief, while on questions of analysis, composition, sources, authorship, date, etc., he is free, independent of tradition, often radical.[54]

In particular, wrote Porter, Bacon appeared reluctant to bring the "religion about Jesus" to the same historical test, or to a test equally historical, as that to which he had subjected the Gospels and the "religion of Jesus." Thus the grammatico-historical method had gone begging in Bacon's description of Paul's religion.

If the "conservatives" were unhappy with Bacon, so were the source-analysts, though for different reasons. In a review of *The Apostolic Message*, E. F. Scott regarded Bacon's idea of the "preacher's anecdotes"[55] as suggestive of Schleiermacher's *Diegesen*-hypothesis, according to which each "stray reminiscence" reflected a sharply defined party with its own Christology and notion of salvation.[56] Stating that the thought of the Church in the earliest period was less diffuse, more general and "naive," Scott concluded that Bacon's theory of anecdotes required inverting. It was the "story" itself, not the mere anecdote or "moral" introduced to illustrate a dogma, which constituted the real point of interest among the earliest Christians.[57] Enslin noted a singular inattention to the lexical in Bacon's *Studies in Matthew*. He wrote that Bacon had not bothered to state which "critical Greek text" of Matthew he had used, though he apparently prized the Western text more highly than did Westcott and Hort.[58] Maurice Goguel wrote that Bacon had not pressed his literary analyses to their proper conclusion, had not inquired, e.g., whether or not those portions of the Fourth Gospel in which another disciple was set above Peter really belonged to the Gospel. Bacon should have determined, Goguel continued, whether or not the redactor's hinting at the Gospel revision by the beloved disciple had influenced passages in which the disciple whom Jesus loved appears. "Would this not also be in order to invoke an especially authorized witness?" asked Goguel. The French scholar maintained that the absence of a proper name elsewhere throughout the Gospel was so unnatural as to suggest its replacement by an anonymity transparent to the Gospel's first readers, and this by conformation to passages in which the beloved disciple appears. At any rate, Goguel concluded that it was not suitable to call the Gospel's redactor the "creator" of the beloved disciple or of the notion that he had revised the Gospel.[59] Howard stated that Bacon's method of approaching the problem of the Fourth Gospel's redaction from the side of the appendix was "decidedly subjective," that his work on John would have been more convincing had he given greater attention to lexical and grammatical details.[60]

Despite the considerable similarities between Bacon's method and that of the form critics, there were just as considerable differences between them. For one thing, Bacon's connection with Schmidt, Dibelius and Bultmann was casual and late. One reason lay in the fact that the First World War had disrupted any real scientific cooperation between America and Germany.[61] In light of Bacon's anti-Wilhelmian stance during World War One, the cynic might suggest he would not have been eager for such cooperation in any event. It is true, of course, that Bacon thoroughly endorsed the Wilson government's declaration of war, interpreting the venture as a consummately moral and religious action on the part of men dedicated to peace.[62] It is also true that he shared his contemporaries' interpretation of Jesus as not countenancing a "non-resistant God,"[63] and fulminated against conscientious objectors.[64] He even compelled a young protegé, leaving the Congregationalist Church for the Society of Friends under strong conviction, to prepare the script of his "Christus Militans."[65] Throughout the war years, however, Bacon never lost admiration for the Holtzmanns and the Harnacks,[66] or for such German immigrants as Francis Lieber, teacher of international law,[67] to say nothing of Baur and Hegel, of which more later.

That which marked the difference between Bacon and members of the form-critical school in Europe was the fact that to the end he was pre-occupied with the New Testament text in its present form, not with the pre-literary, oral stages of the Gospel tradition. Bacon did not deny a period in which oral tradition was the sole vehicle for the transmission of the Gospel record,[68] but he did insist that oral tradition played no real role in the period immediately antecedent to Gospel composition.[69] Since, as he believed, tradition and internal evidence concurred in proving that the sources of our present Gospels were in essence stereotyped written, Greek texts, the notion of *Diegesen* or of oral sources underlying our present Gospels had been demonstrated to be "moribund" and false,[70] and any kindred theory, such as C. C. Torrey's hypothesis of Aramaic originals, fell with the same blow.[71]

To the degree of his preoccupation with source-analysis, Bacon drew fire from the younger generation of critics. On reading *The Story of Jesus and the Beginnings of the Church*, Donald W. Riddle commented that Bacon apparently saw no reason to question the propriety of his own method, that in spite of the work of B. H. Streeter, he still clung to his two-document hypothesis, and that his sole reference to form-critical method was deprecatory. Riddle concluded:

> Surely it may be expected that even such an apotheosis of the Literary-Critical method as this will before long give place to its supplement, the method of interpretation by means of social history.[72]

Another noted that Bacon had made no reference in his *Studies in Matthew* to the *formgeschichtliche* method of investigating the Gospel sources.[73] Werner George Kümmel, in a review of the same volume, reproached Bacon for his assumption that the evangelists had compiled their works solely from written sources, and thus for taking the oral tradition into account only in emergencies. The more disastrous result of this assumption Kümmel located in Bacon's "total misunderstanding of the nature of the early Christian literature," a misunderstanding rooted in Bacon's debates with scholars of a by-gone era and in his neglect of German scholarship. If, Kümmel concluded, Bacon had shared the concerns of contemporary research, he would at least have recognized that the Gospel's situation-in-life was not the polemic intention of the evangelist, but rather the kerygma.[74]

These blows, aimed at Bacon by the sons of the pioneers, are, at the least, delivered "*vom hohen Ross.*" But the description of Bacon as adhering to the two-document hypothesis, in light of a discussion of synoptic sources reminiscent only of an Emanuel Hirsch, is an error, and the conclusion that his disagreement with recent criticism regarding the Petrine character of Mark constitutes a "disparaging word" vis a vis *Formgeschichte* is false.[75] Kümmel's statement to the effect that Bacon did not even put the question as to the soils from which the Gospels emerged and the purpose for which they were transmitted reflects only superficial acquaintance with the Yale scholar's work. Kümmel may be excused, though his own statement regarding the Gospel's situation-in-life is not at all shared by a majority of European scholars, early or late. In Europe, academic custom makes accession to a university chair contingent upon the aspirant's maligning his betters.[76] But Riddle should have known better. Application of social-environmental research — for which the University of Chicago faculty was justly celebrated and which Riddle himself later joined — to the documents of the New Testament and not merely to the historical creeds and confessions of the Church, was engineered principally by Shirley Jackson Case, Bacon's pupil. The irony is that

America's pioneer in form-critical method should have been accused of not employing the very method he pioneered.[77]

Still, as with many a pioneer, the old left its trace, died hard,[78] and Bacon remained committed to a type of source criticism, broadly defined. But to the degree of his divergence from his continental counterparts Bacon deserves acknowledgement as pioneering still another method of biblical research — redactions-criticism.

As early as 1901, Bacon gave notice that he intended not only to pursue literary analysis and the recovery of sources, but also a study of the background and motive of each Gospel and its antecedents.[79] Those who paid him any mind agreed he had been as good as his word. Moffatt and Warren Moulton noted the remarkable approximation of Bacon's researches on Mark's Gospel to those of Albert Loisy. But while the one merely stated such agreement was due to independent research,[80] the other went on in detail to contrast the two scholars as to method and definiteness of application, concluding that though Bacon far exceeded Loisy in the extent to which he found Mark dominated by Paulinism and thus neglected to ascribe as great a creativity to the evangelist as did Loisy, he nevertheless outdid the French scholar in assigning motives for Mark's redactional activity.[81] Fundamental to his five-book theory of Matthew's Gospel, wrote Enslin, was Bacon's contention that Matthew was no mere editor, but in every sense the Gospel's "author."[82] Rawlinson seconded the motion, referring to Bacon's conception of the Gospel evangelist as "much more of an *author*, and much less of a mere scissors-and-paste compiler from sources," as well as to his giving greater attention to the evangelist's redaction and expansion of sources.[83] Ernest Burch commended Bacon for attempting to uncover the mind of "these sympathetic handlers of the tradition," stating that it was inevitable the historical critic should encounter writers indebted to predecessors who transmitted not only what they "received," but also what they offered.[84]

Bacon's pursuit of the evangelists' "method of pragmatic values" furnishes the reader sufficient corroboration of the judgment which his contemporaries placed upon his work as a "redactions-criticism." In light of his uncovering reflections of ritual in the New Testament, it is impossible to concede to the contemporary criticism that Bacon paid no heed to the liturgical custom prevailing in the era of Gospel composition. Krister Stendahl's comparison of Bacon's *Studies in Matthew* with the work of G. D. Kilpatrick[85] led him to state that whereas Bacon could refer to the practice of "targumizing" the gospel, such was purely a category of literature, and to conclude by citing Kilpatrick's statement that Bacon "never treated contemporary liturgical custom as an important element in its production."[86] Bacon's preoccupation with baptism and the Supper as yielding the "two foci" about which the Gospel and Pauline materials were agglutinated gives the lie to such an evaluation. Stendahl, of course, drew his comparison largely for the purpose of indicating the progress which historical criticism had made in the sixteen years between Bacon's and Kilpatrick's volumes on Matthew. Still, such a judgment upon Bacon's research appears to rest upon a severely limited reading of his work. Part of the blame, perhaps, may be laid at the door of Bacon's notorious penchant for leaping into the discussion without preliminary. In any event, the *Studies in Matthew* hardly yield sufficient ground for an appraisal of Bacon's position concerning liturgical deposits.

In his estimate of Bacon's work, Burch felt called upon to add that his method was not new, merely opportunely applied.[87] Nevertheless, Bacon belonged to a circle so small as to deserve a pioneer's credit. At the same time, that circle was large enough to be noticed and thus render current opinion concerning redactions-criticism as a late twentieth-century product a mere prejudice or lapse of memory.

IV: *Nullius Addictus*?

Did Bacon get free, did the use of his method liberate him from the bogey of scribalism, reflected, as he saw it, in the Rabbinism of Princeton or in Ritschlianism's buttressing religion with brute facts? Partial answer to the question is given in Bacon's intense admiration for Baur, whose spirit lurks like Banquo's ghost on almost every page the Yale professor published. The allusions to the Tübingen giant in Bacon's work are too numerous to track, but specific points of contact between them can be readily seen.

Baur, as Bacon, out of sorts with what he had dubbed the "magical" or "teleological" view of Scripture interpretation, called for a method which would permit the scholar to view "innerworldly connections."[88] The German's celebrated "tendency criticism" and its attendant schema issued in a description of Christianity as combining Greek and Jewish elements,[89] as a "spiritual" religion[90] which reached its zenith in the principle of Paulinism for which the Lord is the Spirit, interpreted as "freedom, autonomy and the immediacy of self-consciousness."[91] And, it was Baur who early suggested a pre-Pauline mission and interpreted Stephen's speech in Acts as reflecting the theology of that Hellenistic wing in the Jerusalem church to which Paul was most indebted.[92]

Baur, of course, as did Bacon, located the cause of the division within primitive Christianity in Peter's and his adherents' equivocation concerning Gentile observance of the law in contravention of the apostolic decree,[93] and cited as the first proof of systematic opposition the letters to the Galatians and Corinthians.[94] The Book of Acts, on the other hand, constituted a levelling out of differences between the opposing parties, and credited the universalism achieved by the Church in face of the Gnostic threat along with the Gentile mission to Peter's, not to Paul's account.[95] Baur's discussion of the post-apostolic period as an era in which Jewish-Christianity built upon Pauline soil reads like an early edition of Bacon's description of the regress of religion from Spirit to Book in his *Jesus and Paul*.[96] And for Baur, as for Bacon, the differences between Palestinian and Pauline Christianity had their origin in Jesus' own person.[97]

It was Baur, further, who early advanced the notion of the non-historical character of the Fourth Gospel;[98] described the "beloved disciple" as "John spiritualized," "the highest expression of the Christian consciousness," an ideal,

non-historical figure,[99] and characterized the theology of
that Gospel as emphasizing the person of Jesus as the Logos
become flesh, rather than the death of Jesus with its
vicarious power.[100]

Nor were "reflections of ritual" lost to Baur, though he
insisted the Quartodecimanians agreed with the Synoptists
regarding the day of Jesus' death, having celebrated the
fourteenth of Nisan merely because Jesus had held his last
meal on that day. Bacon had written that the tradition
according to which Jesus died on the fourteenth developed
later and reflected anti-Jewish sentiment. Since the Fourth
Gospel espoused this view, it could not have been written by
an apostle.[101]

Bacon's divergence from Baur was clearest at the point
of the reconciliation of the conflict between Paulinism and
the Jerusalem caliphate. Baur had insisted that harmony
between the antagonists had not been achieved in Paul's lifetime,[102] though with Irenaeus, Tertullian, Clement and
Origen all trace of a breach between Paul and Peter had
disappeared.[103]

The similarities between Bacon and Baur were quickly
detected. Moulton remarked the influence of Baur's
"tendency criticism" on Bacon, agreed that the Gospels
pursued a definite purpose — to that degree Baur's method
retained validity — but added that Bacon's attempt to make
the controversies and institutions of the primitive church the
key to the Gospels' contents was another matter.[104] He also
pointed to the Achilles heel of Baur's method, viz., the
temptation to draw too great a distinction between opposing
parties, to fix questions of date, authorship and literary
relationship upon such a radical differentiation, and thus to
ignore the mixture of disharmonious and disconnected views
and ideas, to say nothing of racial origins, within a given
community.[105] Buchanan, in a burst of sarcasm, wrote that it
had remained to German-American criticism to expose the
untrustworthiness of the apostles and their company,
described Bacon's point as "the old Tübingen fantasia of
Peter and Paul establishing themselves in opposite camps,"
and in a total loss of humor queried:

Are we to take all that German higher critics offer us as Gospel truths, nay, as turning the Gospel truth into untruth, whenever *they* in their omniscience choose to contradict it?[106]

Machen, whose own contact with the Tübingen school had not been at second hand, wrote that no contemporary scholar had been so profoundly influenced by the great Tübingen master as had Bacon,[107] an influence he nevertheless predictably bewailed, contending that Bacon's "neo-Tübingenism" rooted in a radical misinterpretation of Galatians 2:1-10.[108] Gow and Porter directed their criticisms at the end result of Baur's influence, i.e., at Bacon's accenting the Christ of Paul or the "gospel about Jesus" to the disparagement of the "gospel of," Gow affirming that the latter still had priority with the simple and devout,[109] and Porter suggesting that the aesthetic-affectional theology of Jonathan Edwards, with its emphasis upon the Spirit as effecting in us the beauty and truth of Jesus' words and character, furnished the antidote to that far more insecure "religion about Jesus."[110] For Hoskyns as for Buchanan and Machen in their own way, the problem lay not in the emphasis but in the method itself. By fixing the beginning of the Christian religion in the vision of Peter — here, too, Bacon had altered the sketch of Baur who appeared to have robbed Peter in order to pay Paul — Bacon still left unbridged the chasm between the Jesus of history and the Christ of faith, since stress on Peter's vision or on a revelation at the death of a "natural reformer" could never substitute for that larger background to the life and death of the Jesus of history. What is both Pauline and Petrine, Hoskyns declared, also belongs to the teaching of Jesus.[111]

The similarities between Baur and Bacon are unmistakable, but evaluation of the Yale scholar's work can hardly end there. Bacon was dependent upon a scheme, however indirectly mediated, for which another, larger figure than Baur was responsible — Georg Wilhelm Friedrich Hegel, nineteenth century pedagogue to the German world.

On the level of the purely formal, Bacon's productions displayed a veritable riot of triads, suggestive of the Hegelian

movement from pure thought to negation to reconciliation
or sublation in synthesis. Triplicity was assigned to the
career of Jesus. In "phase one," Jesus emerges as prophet,
raising protest on behalf of the "little ones." In "phase two,"
he assumes the title of Christ and undertakes a "national"
ministry. "Phase three" then opens with the temple-
cleansing and concludes with the crucifixion.[112] For Bacon,
the evangelists' Christologies constituted a threesome — the
Markan portrait of the "humble mechanic of Nazareth;" the
apotheosis Christology of Matthew and Luke, and the
Incarnation theology of the Fourth Gospel. Or again, the
Gospels were described as portraying Jesus as the Nazarene
prophet, the Servant and the Son of Man.[113] "What the eye
saw" (Mark), "what the ear heard" (Matthew and Luke), and
"what entered the heart of man" (John), was still another
triad assigned the Gospel accounts. Even Gospel authorship
and composition were conceived in threefold fashion.
"Theologus" (or Strateas" or "A"), nameless elder of
Ephesus and successor of Paul, the "beloved disciple," and
finally the redactor comprise the "author" of the Fourth
Gospel,[114] the three stages of its composition reflected in
festal discourses later expanded into a narrative of Jesus' life
and finally adjusted to synoptic record.[115] The geographical
soils out from which the Gospels emerged and about which
they were arranged were three in number — Palestine
(Galilee-Samaria), Rome and Ephesus. For Bacon, the
entire canon of the New Testament reflected a certain
triplicity, a movement from the "gospel about" to the "gospel
of Jesus" and their synthesis in Pauline-Johannine thought.
The same held true of the history of primitive
Christianity — the Petrine, Jerusalem caliphate
encountered opposition in radical Paulinism, opposition
then yielding to rapprochement in face of the Gnostic threat.
Even world history served up three essential religious
types — Judaism, Hellenism and Christianity. What was
more than these was a mere refraction of one or the other.
And, Christian experience itself was resolved into the triad:
Christ, not-Christ or the believer, and their sublation in the
Christian community.

A three-point sermon does not of necessity root in a notion of the threeness of things, but Bacon's preoccupation with triads throughout his exposition of the New Testament appears too sustained and universal to allow of a merely pragmatic explanation. That riot of triads had Hegel for its father, however indirect the inheritance. It was Hegel for whom triplicity appeared to lie at the very heart of things,[116] and though the Berlin philosopher may have chided his contemporary Schelling for imposing threesomes on anything and everything,[117] in the opinion of his interpreters it was Hegel who exalted the triad to the level of a logical necessity.[118]

If we begin with Bacon's preference for "Spirit" as signalizing the entirety of the divine activity, thus with his understanding of his task as a "phenomenology of Spirit"[119] or a "reading of the Spirit's advance," and if we interpret this pursuit of freedom as coincident with that preference and understanding, then the material agreement between Bacon and Hegelianism, and at the very point where Hegel's logic and phenomenology begin, becomes clear.[120]

The "notion," the "idea," then, whose unfolding constitutes all reality, is Spirit, Spirit interpreted as freedom.[121] Further, and especially important for Hegel and thus for Bacon, freedom is construed not merely as the goal toward which everything moves, but as the *process* or development itself. Thus, Bacon's emphasis upon the "whole" and only the "whole" as Logos or Spirit,[122] and Hegel's insistence upon world history as nothing but "the progress of the consciousness of freedom."[123]

For Hegel, Spirit's first movement toward self-realization, or that movement which thought makes toward its conception of Spirit as self-conscious and self-contained, was a movement in the direction of the contingent, determinate and finite. For Bacon, that contingency or determinateness in which Spirit "negates" itself so as to become concrete, was the Petrine "gospel of Jesus."

We can only be astounded at the degree to which Bacon attempted to trace the whole of the New Testament canon to its Petrine source. At the base of Mark's "original" Gospel

("P") lay the memorabilia of Peter, the present Gospel reflecting Peter's story as it used to be preached by Mark and embellished by a Paulinist. The second synoptic source or "S" Bacon characterized as reminiscences of Jesus' life and ministry sufficient to convey his image as it had impressed Peter and the Zebedees. He explained Matthew's dependence on Mark as due to the latter's authoritatively Petrine character.[124] The same, he contended, was true of Luke whom he described as dependent, at least in part, upon Aramaic, Jerusalemite, Petrine material. Further, it was an interpreter of Peter, among others, who sat for the Fourth Gospel's portrait of the beloved disciple.[125] Bacon's long and tedious arguments in favor of the martyr death of the apostle John and against the historicity of John's Ephesian sojourn — his acceptance of Papias' reference to John's martyrdom, but his rejection of Papias' note concerning the Gospel's publication in John's lifetime; his support of Eusebius' refutation of Irenaeus' notion that John resided in Ephesus and his emendation of the Papias citation in Eusebius so as to remove the apostle and elder from Asia altogether; his attempts to connect the martyred witnesses of Revelation 12:1-3 with James and John, and his minimizing of Papias' and Justin Martyr's endorsement of the Apocalypse[126] — all this maddening and confusing footwork was calculated to fix the Gospel's author(s) as a Jerusalem native, dependent upon the apostles, and ultimately adjusting his account to Petrine tradition in order to secure canonization.[127]

As for Paul, Bacon contended that the apostle's letters were in essence a combination of Petrine and Lyric Wisdom tradition.[128] The Pauline corpus thus furnished another avenue of access to the original, Petrine Gospel.[129]

Bacon was not content with merely tracing literary relationships. He thought he saw the New Testament canon's dependence upon the Petrine "gospel of Jesus" reflected in its theology. Whatever major surgery Mark's final redactor may have performed, the earliest Gospel still contained that portrait of Jesus as Servant against the background of Lyric Wisdom which Bacon believed lay at the heart of Petrine

teaching. The same was true of "S" and its offspring,"Q."
Matthew and Luke revealed traces of the Servant-Wisdom
motif — Matthew in the construction of his five books on
"S's" discourse on filial righteousness,[130] and Luke in the
patterning of his speeches in Acts after the Servant-Wisdom
form.[131] John likewise incorporated Servant material,[132] a
portion of his Christology originating in Palestinian,
Samaritan soil.[133] And it was that concept of forgiveness at
the heart of the doctrine of Christ as Servant, connected with
Peter's "turning again" and coming to focus in the
resurrection appearances, which furnished Paul the gospel
he "received."[134] Behind the two "foci" about which Bacon
saw the Gospel and Pauline materials "agglutinated," lay
Peter's Servant Christology.[135] Indeed, he went so far as to
root Paul's "gospel about Jesus" in Servant-Petrine soil.[136]

Ultimately for Bacon, the Servant motif of Petrine
tradition originated with Jesus himself who in the final phase
of his activity emerged as priest and intercessor, giving
himself for the life of his friends.[137] In Jesus, then, those
components of Jewish martyrology and Lyric Wisdom
which provided the stimulus for Peter's faith, had already
been united.[138]

In such fashion, Bacon painstakingly preserved the
"integrity" of Peter, often in bizarre fashion and frequently
to the total confusion of his readers. But behind the apparent
reduction of Gospel sources to a single, common, Petrine
evangel lay Bacon's conviction that the "idea" must
somehow become concrete, that "Spirit" must become
incarnate. For this reason he conceded greater historical
probability to the figure of the historical Jesus as mediated
through Peter than contemporary criticism could allow.
This "empiricism" of Bacon was often missed. He was rather
accused of agnosticism concerning the historical Jesus,[139] a
curious charge in light of his attacks on the assyriologist
Jensen and Tulane's William Benjamin Smith who had
reduced Jesus to a mere idea,[140] as well as in light of his
ultimate intent to pen a "life."[141] The charge often enough
reflected the critics' inability to distinguish what Bacon
insisted must be kept distinct — the "gospel of" and the

"gospel about Jesus."[142] Where the former or common Gospel was concerned, the emphasis upon its Petrine character was nothing less than a guaranteeing of the historical Jesus, since Petrine tradition had its roots in Jesus himself.

Some regarded this emphasis upon Petrine tradition as reductionism, pure and simple. "We have then only *one* Gospel left," mourned the ever-wary Buchanan,[143] and D. C. Macintosh suggested Bacon had robbed both Jesus and Paul in order to pay Peter.[144] Others appeared to regard the emphasis upon a Petrine core as an alien commitment to the Ur-evangelium hypothesis of Lessing or Herder.[145] Still others praised Bacon for having taken account of "an original common or Catholic faith" without ever knowing why.[146] The majority were confused. Cadbury asked why Bacon never really questioned assigning Mark's oldest material to Peter, or never challenged the identity of the several Marks named in the New Testament.[147] The significance of "S" as further guarantee of the historicity of the "gospel of" was lost to most readers who construed Bacon's idea of the "gospel of the teachings" as a pet hypothesis.[148] They regarded his notion of "S" as a full-blown Gospel as "dangerous reasoning,"[149] or as just one more ingenious notion.[150] Porter's charge that Bacon had not adequately defined the content of "S" was no doubt legitimate.[151] Bacon, indeed, appeared to be calling the scholarly world to substitute the Scylla of "S" for the Charybdis of "Q."[152] But the purpose of "S" did not lie, say, in weaning Luke away from Mark[153] — that was a mere by-product. Back of Bacon's "wandering in a synoptic labyrinth[154] with little more than hypotheses to guide him" lay his "empirical" commitment, his locating the determinateness, contingency and finitude of the idea or "Spirit" in the historical Jesus as conveyed by Petrine tradition.

There was more to Bacon, however, than an "empirical" strain. As earlier intimated,[155] he was not content with what he had uncovered and described as the "gospel of Jesus," and for the reason that it tended to the legal and authoritarian from which he aimed to get free. For Bacon, Matthew and Luke, repristinating the "gospel of" in reaction to the ultra-Paulinism of the completed Mark, represented a type Christianity which established its doctrine on past and external authority, and in the end transformed the Christian message into law. Bacon's description of the legalism in Matthew and Luke, and his characterization of the scribalism into which the post-apostolic age had fallen, served merely to confirm the tendency of the contingent and particular toward authoritarianism. To be sure, the authority of Matthew and Luke was that of the historical Jesus, but that figure as object amenable to criticism was past, external and therefore legal.

Hegel had been of the same mind. The "religious consciousness," bound to events in the life-history of a particular individual, and thus tied to whatever suggestions of externality and finitude such a history might conjure up, for that very reason needed to be transcended, since true freedom owed nothing to external authority or mediation, not even to the authority of the historical Jesus. For Hegel, the ultimate outcome of such a consciousness was "positivity," the heaping up of dogmatic and ritualistic requirements. The early theological writings of Hegel are replete with despair over the pretty pass to which Christendom had come due to its uniting the unchangeable with the changeable in a single historical individual.[156] The "religious consciousness" thus tended to the "bad infinite," to the limiting of the infinite by way of the finite and particular — an unresolved contradiction, a dilemma, a "denial" which somehow had to be denied.

On the other hand, the fact that Hegel and later Bacon accorded what appeared to be an inferior rank to the contingent,[157] did not mean that "Spirit" required no concretizing. On the contrary, it was absolutely necessary that the divine become human — no thinker before or after Hegel had given such wholesale logical and epistemological interpretation to the Incarnation.[158] But, since the Incarnation was necessary, the seeds of that legalistic, positivistic and authoritarian reaction necessarily lay with

Jesus himself, and its husbanding and nourishing in the Matthaean and Lukan "gospel of" equally necessary. Bacon put it simply when he said that a portion of Matthew's legalism rooted in Jesus,[159] and that the Matthaean and Lukan reactions were necessary for the preservation of the story of Jesus' life.[160] With Bacon, the "bad infinite" of the "gospel of" achieved its denial or negation in the "gospel about Jesus." And, since for him, as for Hegel, each stage in the dialectic constituted the sublation or synthesis of what preceded, he described the "gospel of" as containing the seeds of its opposite. Thesis and antithesis were thus present from the very beginning — once more, the Hegel-Baur schema had seen its vindication in the new science of aetiological criticism.[161] If the seeds of the antithesis already lay in the "gospel of Jesus," and thus in the historical Jesus himself, for Bacon, as for Baur, it was Peter who had to furnish the occasion for its historical appearance. To the bafflement of his critics,[162] Bacon separated what he believed Acts 15 had fused,[163] and fixed the occasion for the appearance of the "gospel about" or the "gospel which Paul proclaimed" in Peter's vascillation on the question of eating with Gentiles. Whether originating with Paul himself, or with that pre-Pauline, Hellenistic Christianity on which Bacon later believed Paul came to depend, for him "the gospel about Jesus" represented freedom from the sensuous immediacy of the flesh as past and external authority, and a freedom for communion with an inwardly present Christ.[164]

His critics assumed that Bacon interpreted the gospel of Paul as having emerged without parentage, like Melchizedek, ultimately to be wedded to the "gospel of Jesus" to form a *tertium quid*. For this reason, they accused him of interpreting Paul as an innovator, of leaving the true origins of Paul's religion unexplained,[165] of cutting him adrift from his Jewish heritage,[166] from the historical Jesus[167] and from primitive Christian teaching.[168] Bacon, they allowed, escaped complete scepticism by asserting that the primitive Christology could somehow be disentangled from the Pauline web.[169] For the rest, he had established as little continuity between Jesus and Paul as had Albert Schweitzer.[170]

But again, since for Bacon as for Hegel "what exists must necessarily be contained in the idea,"[171] the Pauline "gospel about" in which the Servant theology was joined to the cosmic Wisdom or Logos interpreted as spiritual principle, as "inwardness," had not emerged by spontaneous generation — its roots also lay in Jesus himself.[172] It had its home, Bacon contended, in historical fact, since the life of Jesus began and ended not merely with the "sayings," but with the "deeds " as well. It opened and closed not only with the "teaching of baptisms" but also with the "teaching of the cup" — the second of the two foci about which Paul's theology centered.[173] Further, however much Paul's doctrine of spiritual union with Christ may have displaced the earlier Jewish martyrology and apocalyptic as reflected in the Petrine Christology, it had its origin in Jesus' own teaching concerning the Spirit.[174]

For Bacon, of course, the story of the development of Christianity could not end with Paul. Though the "gospel about Jesus" had as its goal the transformation of Jesus' death and resurrection as purely "natural" events into phases within the life of a believing community, it nevertheless nursed the tendency toward too drastic a reaction against the common Gospel. The ultra-Paulinism of Mark, with its anti-Semitic, anti-Petrine and antinomian posture, best illustrated the "bad infinite." Mark, wrote Bacon, flagrantly distorted Jesus' position respecting meats, things clean and unclean, and divorce. Indeed, Mark had distorted Jesus' position respecting the law as such. The earliest evangelist (or his redactor) had betrayed an advanced, Gentile-Christian scorn for everything legal.[175]

At this stage in Bacon's dialectic, the critics again raised objections. Moffatt wrote that Bacon's eliminating John Mark from the final edition of the Gospel left him free to assign radical Paulinism to its redactor, "R," and agreed with the "Rabbinist" wing of the History of Religions School that Pfleiderer, Loisy and Bacon had erred in their tendency to read Paul into Mark.[176] Burkitt queried why the Paulinism of Mark could not have been the mind of Christ,[177] and Machen denied all "tendency" to Mark flat outright.[178]

Once more, then, Bacon's detractors had overlooked that fundamental, Hegelian commitment in him, the notion that the "whole is the Logos," that each stage in the dialectic is overcome only in the sense that it forms the necessary condition for what follows, and is thus not overcome at all. To that extent, at least, Mark had not "obscured" the historical tradition, and to that extent his Jesus was the Jesus of Galilee.[179]

The synthesis, for Bacon, was no merger of unrelated opposites, but merely the sublation (Hegel had used the term *Aufhebung*) or re-combination of its conditions or predecessors, each of which contained the other as its negation or denial. "Spirit" had achieved its consciousness in the rapprochement between "the gospel of" and the "gospel about Jesus." Paul had labored to effect the synthesis — here lay the difference between Baur and Bacon — but the greater, deeper work remained to the Ephesian evangelist.[180] The fact that Bacon interpreted the First Epistle of Peter as the canonical symbol of that rapprochement (and Nicea as its ecclesiastical symbol)[181] is suggestive of the degree to which he regarded the synthesis as contained in the original notion or idea. In one way or another, Peter lay at the bottom of it all, or rather, the reconciliation of opposites was effected by the historical Jesus who had bridged the gulf between the "teachings" by electing and then abandoning the Galilean gospel, first for the proclamation of himself as Messiah, then for the idea of his death as intercession, as sacrifice.

According to Bacon, it was this synthesis — recognized through the genetic method and the "appreciation of differences"[182] — which constituted Christianity the "ultimate world religion."[183] Taking a leaf from Hegel, in the union of the "gospel of" and the "gospel about," the "notion" or "idea," having confronted itself with the finite, external and alien, had overcome and preserved all these phases so as to emerge as "Spirit" — the only reality, infinite, its own result, self-conscious and self-contained.

According to Hegel, man may do nothing *to* Spirit as the idea's final realization, may do nothing *for* Spirit. Nothing may be imposed on Spirit *ab extra*, and for the simple reason that whatever appears to be brought to Spirit from the outside is Spirit's own doing, its own positing of the "other" and the other's motion or pressure. The confrontation of Spirit with its opposite was thus a mere pretence, an illusion,[184] and the entire movement of the idea a *Spiel* or game.[185] Yet, the existence of the world, and thus of nature and history, was not gratuitous — Spirit requires the world to achieve its self-consciousness. Consequently, for Hegel, thought, philosophizing, logic, consists in merely tracing, observing or noting down Spirit's coming to being in the world.[186] Herein lay the empiricism of Hegel — method was all-important, and the truth a way.

Bacon's assertion that he was not a theologian but rather a "critic," one who read the Spirit's "advance," and his perennial surprise at being attacked for grafting alien and foreign stuff onto the Gospel tree, suggests that his head was turned in the same direction.

Since nothing is done to Spirit which it does not do to itself, by itself, logic can only be the Spirit's own advance in the realm of thought; external nature its own advance in space, and history the Spirit's own advance in time. Then, explanations of that advance which appeal to the transcendent or eschatological, the prodigious or miraculous, are from the outset ruled out. Hegel was not a pantheist in any ordinary sense of the term — in his description of the "religious consciousness," he referred to man's distance from God as a genuine and cruelly painful sense of alienation — but Hegel did not give finality to man's distance from God.[187] In the synthesis, the alienation was overreached, demoted to the status of a condition, a presupposition. Herein lay the "idealism" or better, the rationalism of Hegel.[188] The divine's transcendence over the human thus fell within human experience.[189] Immanence, then, properly characterized the existence of the divine. For this reason, Hegel rejected the teleological view, at least as expounded by the majority of his contemporaries, according to which purpose is introduced from without, not as indwelling and internal.[190] It was mechanism which supplied the appropriate explanation to natural and human occurrence — which meant that the miraculous as prodigy was excluded.[191]

Eschatology and apocalyptic received a similar treatment with Bacon. His insistence upon immanence, continuity and uniformity as marking the divine,[192] and his subsequent refusal to assign apocalyptic ideas to the historical Jesus,[193] seen e.g., in his "genealogy" of the abomination-sayings[194] and vigorously challenged by his critics,[195] may have had little to do with Hegelian reaction against teleology. His interpretation of the history of Israel as an advance,[196] and his preoccupation with a "spiritual evolution" toward a manhood conceivably transcending the life "hid with Christ in God,"[197] may be less a reflection of his commitment to a kind of entelechy than to Darwinism and modern theories of progress. At the same time, as with Hegel,[198] Bacon's notion of man's spiritual advance was not that of an uninterrupted development — the priestly document represented a decline in the religion and morals of Judaism;[199] the post-apostolic period a fall from the religion of the Spirit to that of the Book, and the "bad infinite" or "unhappy consciousness" inherent in the Princeton and Ritschlian theologies called for its sublation in a new spiritual consciousness. Further, Bacon gave as little attention to the theories of biological evolution as did Hegel to the theories of evolution current in his time,[200] though Darwinism would not have been incompatible with the thought of either one. Bacon, of course, did entertain the idea that the species had reached its biological apogee. Yet, this did not constitute an alien commitment to the notion of the Puritan frontiersmen as the *Herrenvolk*. If we allow Hegel one hundred years to ripen and transport him, nervously handled by scores of interpreters, across the Atlantic to a spot east of the Alleghenies, he might look much as he appears in Benjamin Bacon. The similarities between Bacon and e.g., Josiah Royce, the Harvard thinker, were not coincidental. Both, it could be argued, met Hegel through intermediaries, the one through Baur and the other through Charles Saunders Peirce. Only a few like William James had lived long enough in Europe to tackle the

Phenomenologie des Geistes in the original, and James confessed to having little appetite for Hegel.

If Bacon had little patience with eschatology, at least of the "consequent" or thorough-going variety, miracle as the heralding of the new wrought from outside nature and history got as little attention from him, and again for the reason that immanence, not intervention, had to mark the presence of the divine.[201] The most thaumaturgic traits in Mark's Gospel were thus expunged;[202] the resurrection narratives in Matthew and Luke were attributed to a "materialism" rooting in the Jewish hope,[203] and, together with the story of the Virgin Birth, were reinterpreted in terms of the believer's own "spiritual" birth and resurrection.[204] The only exception to Bacon's hermeneutic were Jesus' miracles of healing. They, he asserted, were authentic.[205] Bacon thus took his seat in that great throng of adherents of the History of Religions School which allowed the credibility of the exorcisms because they admitted of an explanation in accord with modern theories of the human psyche.

In the final analysis, however, it was not a modern world-view which induced Bacon to "spiritualize" or "demythologize" the miracle stories of the New Testament. It was Hegel, or rather, Hegelianism. Bacon's reinterpretation of the miracles in terms of the believer's existence had its foundation in the idea that the figure of the Christ involved, indeed, demanded its "complement" in a community.[206] Above all, it required that complement in order to preserve contemporaneity with what would otherwise have become mere past — the life of Christ.[207] Since, therefore, the Absolute had put aside the trammels of the sensuous to achieve resurrection in the experience of the community, and since the Logos-Spirit was the "whole" and only the "whole" — Christ *and* "the man that is to be"[208] — then what was true of Christ must be true also of the believer. When, in a final criticism of his old friend's preoccupation with the "gospel about," Frank Porter scribbled, "really our self is Christ," he had little idea how close he had come to the heart of his colleague's thought.[209]

Bacon of course, could speak of "laws," laws of nature and history and human life.[210] Hegel could do the same, but that "tranquil kingdom of laws" was the abiding place of mere scientific "understanding," of formal thought — a notion reminiscent of Plato's concept of διάνοια as something short of complete knowledge.[211] And, since "understanding"constituted a "bad infinite" by merely re-describing the things men want *explained* and thus by pronouncing a benediction on the status quo, scientific understanding with its attendant laws had to give way to self-consciousness at home in "reason" and its more fluid forms. There is but a short step from Bacon's emphasis upon Spirit as the "whole" to an interpretation of Spirit as merely implicit in law. It was Bacon's way of getting free of the perennial embarrassment into which the "orthodox" fall by conceding the current world-view, then, inhibited and frustrated in their attempts to perforate it so as to allow room for the divine, cry foul. Bacon's contemporaries construed the universe as a closed continuum. He was willing to concede the notion, provided Spirit was understood as making up the whole, but when his commitment to Spirit was forgotten and he refused to allow a mere puncturing of the alleged continuum, his critics charged him with "anti-supernaturalism" and psychologizing, with "naturalism," "pragmatism" and denial of the Scripture's inspiration.[212]

In the end, what rendered Bacon captive was what he most shared with Hegel — belief in rationality. It is well enough known that for Hegel religious faith was but a half-way house between unreflected consciousness and rational insight. Because reason was "sovereign of the world" and world-history a rational process,[213] God could be reached by way of speculative knowledge.[214] Now the content of that knowledge might be identical with the content of revelation, but since the latter had not yet overcome finiteness with pure self-consciousness, it could not be the savior and salvation of men. That exalted status remained to philosophy alone. Hegel may have begun with Kant's notion of the "practical reason" as independent of contingent circumstance,[215] but by uncompromisingly holding to the idea that since the being of God consists in self-consciousness[216] he must ultimately be known via rational insight, he harked back to a metaphysic far behind that of Kant.

The same presupposition underlay Bacon's work, and the evidence is to be found in Hegel's and thus in Bacon's confidence in method. Hegel, as many of his contemporaries, was fascinated with the developing natural sciences. What intrigued him, however, was not so much the content those sciences yielded, as the method by which they obtained their results.[217] Why could not scientific method be universally applied? After a bit of minor surgery which should prevent his "notion" or "idea" from degenerating into the mere "type" or "genus" of the natural sciences and thus render it capable of protecting the concrete and particular, Hegel proceeded to the application of the new method to consciousness, logic, natural history, law, aesthetics and history. And since *Geist, Pneuma*, Spirit, consciousness, God, lay at the heart of it all, recognition of Spirit as the creative potency in the world-drama could come only through the means appropriate to it — thought, reflection, ratiocination. For Hegel, that meant only one thing — use of method. Dialectic was the thing by which to catch self-consciousness, independent and regnant. And since reflection thus defined was reserved to those eras in which Minerva's owl had already taken flight; since thought had to stand at the finish-line in order to see what led up to it, reflection was reserved for the thinker, not the doer, whose will the "cunning of reason" had stirred up to be its (unreflective) instrument or tool. The intellectual hybris in Hegel's system is only the result of his insistence upon the exercise of reason as yielding self-consciousness.

With much less sophistication, Bacon's confidence in "aetiological method" together with its uncovering of "pragmatic values,"[218] and its corollary in the "appreciation of differences" as yielding a vision of Spirit as beginning, process and goal, reflected the same commitment to rationality. There really was no modesty in Bacon's refusal to be dubbed a theologian, any more than there was humility in Hegel's refusal to wear the title "historian." If things and events, whether of history as a whole or of primitive Christianity, enjoyed such dialectical relation to each other, independent of manipulation and arrangement, what remained was merely to note, mark and observe such a state of affairs. If history is theodicy, there is nothing for it but to "tell it like it is."[219] Use aetiological method and share the cosmic potency!

In Germany, romantic reaction to such intellectualism was swift in coming. Goethe, Schleiermacher, the revival of Roman Catholicism, aspects of the French revolution, Pietism and the Awakening all reflected a refusal to acknowledge reason as the essence of the divine or human. Hegel himself may have contributed to that reaction. It was he, after all, who assigned *Gemüt* to the Germanic world, a "heart" which, wedded to the "objective" in Christianity rendered that world the bearer of the higher principle of Spirit.[220] And in this country, current reaction against materialism, and the embracing of romantic idealism have their stimulus, if not their reason, in the kind of intellectualism Bacon purveyed.

One of Hegel's hard sayings is that the "rational is the real, and the real the rational," or that "reason is the substantial basis of consciousness, as well as of the external and natural."[221] The force, if not the exact meaning of this saying is that the existence of the contingent is not gratuitous, but is required by Spirit for its realization. Yet, Hegel was forced to qualify such statements. The real or actual did not *always* achieve full presence in a given moment.[222] The relation between the real and the sensuous, the palpable and contingent, was not *always* reciprocal. Many contingents could fall short of reality. Indeed, much in the world had to fall short of an epiphany of Spirit, or it would have been all over with Hegel's dialectic. And to the degree he agreed that not every moment could see the realization of the Absolute, to that degree he paved the way for his "left wing," for Strauss and Sterner and Bruno Bauer, and sacrificed particularity and contingency to the idea-universal, no matter how upset he pretended to be with the natural sciences which cared only for types. For Bacon,

Christ was the "supreme teacher of humanity,"[223] the
"Redeemer,"[224] conscious of his Messiahship and sonship.
He wrote that if another should arise, equally qualified to be
the leader of humanity toward its goal of sonship and
brotherhood, his authority would only be a second —
leadership would remain with Jesus.[225] Jesus, his
existence, death and resurrection, were thus "necessary" to
Spirit. On the other hand, since the events recorded in the
Bible constitute only a segment of the "spiritual evolutionary
process,"[226] the sufferings of Christ could not be complete
without the "lesser martyrdoms" of his "complement."[227]
Bacon was not thinking here of the "Body of Christ"
construed as corporate personality, but of the idea-universal
and its relation to the single instance. If the Spirit is the
whole, no matter how those sufferings may appear preserved
in their particularity, in the ultimate they cannot resist
sublation in the "idea" of suffering, cannot resist re-
combination in a speculative Good Friday. And, despite
Jesus' consciousness of prophethood (not intending to be the
founder of a new religion but, as Schelling put it, having
become its "content"), might not he along with Napoleon,
that "World-Spirit on horseback," together with a host of
others, be reduced to the tool of reason's "cunning" — his
will, his mission, no doubt arising out of a single-minded
reading of events, but himself unconscious of its relation to
the whole? To the degree of Bacon's infatuation with the
"whole," to that degree he was liable to the same fault as he
had uncovered in Josiah Royce's idea of the "beloved
community," viz., that it gave assent to formulations in
which "the mystical body is everything and the Head of the
body disappears . . . altogether."[228] Rationality had
rendered Jesus the archetypal, ideal man, a "representation
of the divine idea."[229]

That preoccupation with the idea-universal, with
"Spirit," its "reading" or perceiving construed as freedom,
freedom guaranteed to a method which assumed that
consciousness of the object and consciousness of the self
were one and the same, led Bacon at least to the brink of
reducing faith to an exercise of the mind. In this respect,

perhaps, he differed little from his "orthodox" critics who regarded the Bible as a quarry from which to mine facts in support of dogmas requiring mental assent.

Bacon's perennial drumming away at "inwardness"[230] as the mark or sign of an existence which furnished Christ his "complement" for the sake of which events in Jesus' life were interpreted as realized in that of the believer,[231] was not a concession to Pietism. That inwardness could only be the obverse side of rationality. For Bacon, it was reason governed spiritual reality. As Hegel had written, "the last summit of inwardness is thought."[232] This view of rationality as the proper business of faith led Bacon to relegate what lay at the heart of the Pauline "gospel about" to the merely contingent — Paul's concept of grace. Some of Bacon's critics noted the curious irony in his abandoning what he appeared most intent on preserving,[233] though from the standpoint of their own presuppositions, it was a case of the kettle calling the pot black. Nevertheless, Bacon's description of the Pauline law-grace dilemma as rooted in historical accident[234] indicates to what degree he had intellectualized the Christian religion, and in the end missed what for Paul and the remainder of the New Testament spells man's true freedom — the sovereign favor of God by which He grants life without exacting conditions.

For Hegel, grace could not be supreme, not when man's existence centered in his head, not when Spirit required elevation to the level of self-consciousness through an effort of the mind. And, because Bacon could not allow the supremacy of grace, but reduced its proclamation to the level of a subject which existed merely to be taken up into the predicate; reduced its concrete demonstration in the death of Christ to the level of the contingent which existed merely to be absorbed into the whole, and because he assumed that whole to be disclosed to consciousness or rationality, he got free of scribalism, only to swear fealty to a master equally as tyrannical — the self.

In the last analysis, however, though his method may have been only a means to that which in the end eluded him, it was Bacon's method, not his theology which rendered him founder and pioneer.

1. Rudolf Schnackenburg, *The Gospel According To St. John*, trans. Kevin Smyth (New York: Herder and Herder, 1968), I, p. 209.

2. Cf. *The Journal of Religion*, VI (1926), p. 330; *Theologische Literaturzeitung*, XXXVI (1911), p. 297; *The Expository Times*, XLII (1931), p. 268; E. C. Hoskyns, *The Fourth Gospel*, ed. Francis Noel Davey (London: Faber and Faber, 1947), p. 38; W. F. Howard, *The Fourth Gospel in Recent Criticism and Interpretation*, revised by C. K. Barrett (London: The Epworth Press: 1961), pp. 29, 32; Adolf Jülicher, *Einleitung in das Neue Testament*, 7te Auflage (Tübingen: J. C. B. Mohr, 1931), p. 22; *Theologische Rundschau*, XV (1912), p. 283; James Moffatt, "Professor B. W. Bacon," *The Expository Times*, XLIII (1932), p. 442; *The Hibbert Journal*, XXIX (1930 - 1931), p. 574. The works cited here correspond to the names cited above.

3. *The American Journal of Theology*, XIV (1910), p. 157, and A. J. Grieve, review of *Studies in Matthew*, *The Congregational Quarterly*, IX (1931), p. 89.

4. Cf. E. F. Scott, "The New Criticism of the Gospels," *The Harvard Theological Review*, XIX (1926), p. 152.

5. *Ibid.*, p. 155.

6. Cf. Dennis Nineham, *The Gospel of St. Mark*, *The Pelican Gospel Commentaries*, (New York: The Seabury Press, 1968), p. 394f.

7. Cf. Werner Georg Kümmel, review of *Studies in Matthew*, *Theologische Literaturzeitung*, LVII (1932), p. 30.

8. Note the remarks of an old pupil, Robert C. Calhoun in Bainton, p. 218.

9. In a review of Bacon's volume on Munger, Preserved Smith suggested that lack of soul was the price Bacon paid for his haste to see himself in print, cf. *The Harvard Theological Review*, VIII (1915), p. 147.

10. Moffatt, p. 441.

11. Howard, p. 31.

12. Cf. Pere Lagrange's reference to Bacon's scorn for Roman Catholic works on the Gospel of Mark in *Revue Biblique*, XXXV (1926), p. 312.

13. James Drummond, review of *The Fourth Gospel in Research and Debate*, *The Hibbert Journal*, IX (1910), p. 195.

14. Gerald Burney Smith of Chicago saw plainly enough Bacon's aversion to the legalism of the prevailing Continental theology, and described his *Christianity Old and New* as calling for an advance beyond the severely ethical boundaries of Ritschlian interpretation, cf. *The American Journal of Theology*, XIX (1915), p. 142.

15. *Theodore Thornton Munger*, p. 230.

16. Cf. p. 8 above.

17. Cf. *The Apostolic Message*, p. 40.

18. Cf. F. C. Burkitt, *The Earliest Sources for the Life of Jesus* (London: Constable and Co., 1910), p. 48; J. Gresham Machen, review of *Jesus and Paul*, *The Princeton Theological Review*, XIX (1921), p. 687; Harris Franklin Rall, review of *The Apostolic Message*, *The Journal*

of Religion, VI (1926), p. 434; John Mackay, review of *The Story of Jesus and the Beginnings of the Church, The Princeton Theological Review,* XXVI (1928), p. 300; A. E. J. Rawlinson, review of *Studies in Matthew, The Church Quarterly Review,* CXIII (1931 - 1932), p. 112.

19. Albert Schweitzer, *Geschichte der Leben-Jesu Forschung,* 6te Auflage (München: Siebenstern Taschenbuch Verlag, 1966), II, 586.

20. On occasion, Bacon seemed to relish the title "modernist," cf. *Christianity Old and New,* p. 32.

21. From the unpublished notes of Frank Chamberlain Porter and D. C. Macintosh's review of *Christianity Old and New, Yale Review,* IV (1915), p. 431.

22. Amos N. Wilder, *Eschatology and Ethics in the Teaching of Jesus* (New York: Harper and Brothers, 1950), pp. 154, 156, 158; cf. Kümmel, p. 31.

23. From the unpublished notes of Frank Chamberlain Porter.

24. Ernest W. Burch, "The Jesus of the Gospels," *The Journal of Religion,* XI (1931), p. 446.

25. Henry J. Cadbury, p. 328f.

26. *Jesus The Son of God,* p. ix.

27. *The Gospel of Mark,* p. viii.

28. *Ibid.*

29. "History and Dogma in John," p. 114.

30. *The Spectator,* XC (1905), p. 444f.

31. Machen, p. 687; cf. also Machen's review of *He Opened To Us The Scriptures, The Princeton Theological Review,* XXI (1923), p. 640.

32. Henry Gow, review of *The Story of Jesus and the Beginnings of the Church, The Hibbert Journal,* XXVI (1927-1928), p. 557, and Mackay, p. 300.

33. E. S. Buchanan, review of *Is Mark a Roman Gospel? Bibliotheca Sacra,* LXXVII (1920), p. 118.

34. Delia Bacon, *The philosophy of the plays of Shakspere unfolded* (London: 1857).

35. Moffatt, p. 438.

36. Joseph Louis Perrier, review of *The Founding of the Church, The Journal of Philosophy,* VII (1910), p. 250.

37. *The Athenaeum,* 4316 (1910), p. 64.

38. J. M. Thompson, review of *Christianity Old and New, The Hibbert Journal,* XV (1914 - 1915), p. 227.

39. *The Times Literary Supplement* (January 14, 1926), p. 20.

40. From the unpublished notes of Frank Chamberlain Porter.

41. J. Gresham Machen, review of *Is Mark a Roman Gospel? The Princeton Theological Review,* XX (1922), p. 327.

42. E. S. Buchanan, review of *The Gospel of Mark, The Expository Times,* XXXVII (1925 - 1926), p. 63f.

43. E. S. Buchanan, review of *Is Mark a Roman Gospel?* p. 118.

44. Lagrange, p. 314.

45. *The Athenaeum,* p. 63f.

46. Cf. p. 61 above; *The Fourth Gospel in Research and Debate*, pp. 133, 221, 485; "Pauline Elements in the Fourth Gospel. I," pp. 208f., 211, 219, 223; "Pauline Elements in the Fourth Gospel. II. Parables of the Shepherd," *Anglican Theological Review*, XI (1920), p. 319; "Tatian's Rearrangements of the Fourth Gospel," *The American Journal of Theology*, IV (1900), p. 771; *An Introduction to the New Testament*, p. 274; "Immortality in the Fourth Gospel," p. 293; "The Motivation of John 21:15 - 25, pp. 71, 73; "Sources and Method of the Fourth Evangelist," p. 119f.; *The Gospel of the Hellenists*, pp. 403, 405.

47. Cf. *The Fourth Gospel in Research and Debate*, p. 455.

48. Meyer, p. 286.

49. Cf. *Revue Biblique*, XXIX (1920), p. 144, and XLIII (1934), p. 306.

50. *Revue Biblique*, XXIX (1920), p. 143.

51. Cf. Hoskyns, p. 37.

52. A. M. Hunter, *Interpreting the New Testament 1900 - 1950* (Philadelphia: Westminster Press, 1951), p. 84.

53. Letters of Principal James Denney to W. R. Nicoll, cited in W. F. Howard, p. 2.

54. From the unpublished notes of Frank Chamberlain Porter.

55. According to Bacon, those sayings and incidents from which the Gospel sources were ultimately derived, cf. pp. 72ff.

56. In light of Bacon's clear delineation of his position over against the oral-Gospel hypothesis, this statement of Scott was an error, cf. p. 98 below.

57. E. F. Scott, pp. 156, 160ff.

58. Morton Scott Enslin, "The Five Books of Matthew," *The Harvard Theological Review*, XXIII (1931), pp. 94ff.

59. Maurice Goguel, "La formation de la tradition johannique d'apres B. W. Bacon," *Revue d'Histoire et de Philosophie Religieuses*, XIV (1934), pp. 434f., 438.

60. Howard, pp. 98f., 117.

61. *The Gospel of Mark*, p. viii.

62. "If we enter the bloody arena . . . we shall stand for 'the gospel of peace'." "The Epistle of Moral Preparedness," p. 479; "America, the late-comer, has been brought into the war by the appeal of moral ideas. . . . Only one thing . . . could drag the country out . . . that was pacifism itself. . . . Americans are pacifists to the bone . . . we are 'fighting for peace'. . . . We could not be driven to fight by any less urgent motive. . . . It is said to be 'democracy' for which the world is agonizing today; but if so it is a kind of democracy which reaches a higher level than the ideals of the practical politicians — the level of religion," "Christ and the Pacifist," *Yale Review*, VII (1918), pp. 293f., 295, 304; "It is not enough for the Christian merely 'to do nothing contrary to the law of love'; he must actively toil and suffer in its service, fighting to the death," "Non-Resistance: Christian or Pagan?" p. 79; "The time may be long in coming, but if Jesus be *the Christ*, sooner or later the allegiance to him will bring men into conflict

with political powers that are based on principles diametrically opposed to his," "Christus Militans," p. 547.

63. "Jesus teaches *unlimited* non-resistance where only personal and selfish interests are at stake; but resistance unto blood for the sake of the Kingdom," "Non-Resistance: Christian or Pagan?" p. 80.

64. "Let the religious leaders of our great half-organized democracy ask themselves soberly whether Christianity has nothing better to give in this world-crisis than sentimentality linking hands with fanaticism. . . . Shall we see the spectacle of 'conscientious objectors' to military service plotting to assassinate by poison their country's noblest, most devoted patriot, shall we hear silly doctrines of non-resistance imputed to men who 'resisted unto blood striving against sin' and shall we have no representative, united effort from the Church to mobilize the moral forces of Christendom?" "The Epistle of Moral Preparedness," p. 479; "Will (Christianity) kindle the spirit and nerve the arm of those who are dying to make way for liberty, or will it preach a doctrine of non-resistance that no logic, lay or clerical, can make other in its issue than disloyal surrender of the cause of justice, humanity, and the kingdom of God?" Christ and the Pacifist," p. 305.

65. From a conversation with Roland H. Bainton, New Haven, Connecticut, 1965.

66. Cf. "Imperialism and the Christian Ideal," p. 470.

67. "Liberty Not Stone Dead in Germany," *The New York Times Magazine* (July 29, 1917), p. 15.

68. *The Development of the Synoptic Tradition,* p. 71.

69. *Ibid.*

70. Cf. note 56 above.

71. *The Gospel of Mark,* pp. 58ff.

72. Donald W. Riddle, review of *The Story of Jesus and the Beginnings of the Church, The Journal of Religion,* VII (1927), p. 471.

73. A. J. Grieve, p. 88.

74. Kümmel, p. 31.

75. Cf. *The Story of Jesus and the Beginnings of the Church,* p. 136 — the passage referred to in Riddle's review.

76. Cf. e.g., Willi Marxsen's charge that though form-criticism should logically have preceded redactions-criticism, earlier generations of scholars lacked the courage to carry their research to its proper conclusion — a specious attack, in light of the form-critical pioneer's acceptance of the investigations of Wellhausen, Weiss, Schweitzer and of Bacon as thus far adequate to represent the individuality and theological creativity of the Gospel writers. Willi Marxsen, *Mark the Evangelist,* trans. Roy A. Harrisville et al (Nashville: Abingdon Press, 1969), p. 22. Cf. also Rudolf Bultmann, *Die Geschichte der synoptischen Tradition,* 4te Auflage, (Göttingen: Vandenhoeck und Ruprecht, 1958), Teil III.

77. If Fr. Jose O'Callighan had actually discovered an extract of Mark's Gospel among the Qumran scrolls, and thus advanced by twenty years

the date of the Gospel's composition, Bacon, like others, would no doubt have been accused of being too little preoccupied with source-analysis, and too much with "aetiological criticism" and the "method of pragmatic values."

78. Cf. e.g., Eduard Schweizer's criticism of both Bultmann and Bacon as attempting to solve the problem of the Johannine literature by literary means in, *Ego Eimi*. Die religionsgeschichtliche Herkunft und theologische Bedeutung der johanneischen Bildreden (Göttingen: Vandenhoeck und Ruprecht, 1965), p. 108. Krister Stendahl, after examining the formula-quotations in Matthew, concluded that though they provide a key to the character and milieu of the Gospel, they could not be assigned to a special written source (Bacon's "N") but rather to oral traditions or "memoranda" handled freely by the evangelist. Cf. Stendahl, *The School of St. Matthew* (Philadelphia: Fortress Press, 1968, reprint), pp. 20, 151, 203f.

79. "Ultimate Problems of Biblical Science," *passim*.

80. James Moffatt, "B. W. Bacon, The Beginnings of Gospel Story," *The Hibbert Journal*, VIII (1909), p. 226.

81. Warren J. Moulton, "The Relation Of The Gospel Of Mark To Primitive Christian Tradition," *The Harvard Theological Review*, III (1910), pp. 423ff.

82. Enslin, p. 77.

83. A. E. J. Rawlinson, p. 111.

84. Ernest W. Burch, p. 445f. In this article, Burch had written that Bacon's *Jesus the Son of God* would stand as a contribution to the American type of form-criticism, cf. p. 92 above. The comments of Burch and Rawlinson are, however, reminiscent of Marxsen's criticism of Dibelius as reducing the author-evangelist to the level of a mere collector, cf., Marxsen, p. 15f.

85. George Dunbar Kilpatrick, *The origins of The Gospel according to St. Matthew* (Oxford: At the Clarendon Press, 1946).

86. Stendahl, pp. 20, 151, 203f.; cf. Kilpatrick, p. 78.

87. Burch, p. 446.

88. Ferdinand Christian Baur, *Das Christentum und Die christliche Kirche der Drei ersten Jahrhunderte*, 2te, Neu Durchgearbeitete Ausgabe (Tübingen: Verlag und Druck von L. Fr. Fues, 1860), I, 6.

89. *Ibid.*, p. 16.

90. *Ibid.*, p. 8.

91. *Ibid.*, p. 61.

92. *Ibid.*, pp. 42f., 131, 136. It was Baur, incidentally, who first suggested the literary relationship between the record of Stephen's death and the passion history, cf. *ibid.*, p. 42, and Bacon, "Stephen's Speech," p. 215f.

93. Baur, pp. 51, 103.

94. *Ibid.*, pp. 53, 57f.

95. *Ibid.*, pp. 126f., 104f.

96. *Ibid.*, p. 107.

97. *Ibid.,* p. 47.

98. *Ibid.,* p. 24.

99. *Ibid.,* pp. 24, 170.

100. *Ibid.,* p. 171.

101. *Ibid.,* pp. 160ff.

102. *Ibid.,* pp. 53, 141; cf., pp. 12, 22. For Baur, the apostle John had been leader of the anti-Pauline movement in Ephesus, *ibid.,* p. 82.

103. *Ibid.,* p. 142.

104. Moulton, p. 431f.

105. *Ibid.,* p. 430.

106. Buchanan, review of *Is Mark a Roman Gospel?* pp. 116, 118.

107. Machen, review of *Jesus and Paul,* p. 686f.

108. Machen, review of *Is Mark a Roman Gospel?* p. 326f.

109. Gow, p. 558.

110. From the unpublished notes of Frank Chamberlain Porter.

111. Edwin C. Hoskyns, review of *The Story of Jesus and the Beginnings of the Church, Theology,* XVII (1928), p. 174f.

112. Cf. pp. 79f. above.

113. Cf. pp. 78f. above.

114. Cf. p. 61 above.

115. Cf. p. 61 above.

116. Cf. G. R. C. Mure, *The Philosophy of Hegel* (London: Oxford University Press, 1965), p. 39. Hegel could put it theologically: "God is known only as Spirit when He is recognized as triune. This new principle is the hinge on which world history turns. History begins and ends here," G. W. F. Hegel, *Philosophie Der Geschichte* (Stuttgart: Philipp Reclam Jun., 1961), p. 440. This and subsequent translations of the *Philosophie* are the author's.

117. Cf. J. N. Findlay, *Hegel, A Re-Examination,* Third Impression (London: Allen and Unwin, 1970), p. 87.

118. *Ibid.,* p. 81. Findlay, one of the most skilled of Hegel's present day interpreters, first denied the term "method" to Hegel's triadic formulations, arguing that they merely confused the course of his thought and were the source of all that was unpersuasive and unintelligible. He later retracted this opinion and admitted that Hegel's "dialectical method" represented a "higher-level comment" on notions and positions previously entertained, cf. *ibid.,* p. 353 and the supplementary note on p. 354.

119. Cf. p. 9 above.

120. "'Spirit' (is) the central notion in terms of which (Hegel's) system may be understood. . . . Hegel's dialectical method (is) unintelligible without the notion of Spirit. . . . The crowning point in the notion of Spirit is that it is . . . the *only* or the *absolute* reality, that it is what Hegel calls 'the True,' or the 'Truth' of everything. . . . It is in Spirit that we see the fully carried out meaning of the Idea," Findlay, pp. 35, 46, 288.

121. "The substance, the essence of Spirit is freedom. . . . Freedom is the sole truth of Spirit. . . . Spirit . . . does not have unity outside itself, but has already found it; it is in and for itself. . . . Spirit is existence for itself (*Bei-sich-selbst-sein*). Precisely this is freedom. . . ." Hegel, p. 58f.; cf. p. 60.

122. Cf. p. 9 above.

123. Hegel, pp. 61, 605; cf. p.137: "What Spirit is it always was in itself. The distinction is only the development of this self-contained existence. . . . The stages which Spirit appears to have behind it, it has also in the depths of its present." Cf. also Findlay, p. 288: "Spirit . . . is . . . its own result: 'it itself brings itself forth out of the presuppositions it makes for itself — out of the Logical Idea and external Nature — and is the truth as much of the one as of the other.'"

124. Cf. p. 45 above.

125. Cf. *The Gospel of the Hellenists,* p. 240.

126. Cf. p. 60f. above. Bacon virtually exhausted the topic in the following: "Recent Aspects of the Johannine Problem. — I. The External Evidence," p. 530f.; "In My Father's House are Many Mansions," p. 478; "The Anti-Marcionite Prologue to John," pp. 43f., 46f., 49f., 54; "Marcion, Papias, and 'The Elders'," pp. 139, 144f., 156f., 159; "The Elder John in Jerusalem," pp. 194, 197, 199; "An Emendation of the Papias Fragment," pp. 176, 178, 181; "The Elder of Ephesus and the Elder John," p. 125; "Gospel Criticism and Christian Origins," p. 619; "The Elder John, Papias, Irenaeus, Eusebius and the Syriac Translator," pp. 4f., 8, 15, l9ff.; "Papias and the Gospel According to the Hebrews," p. 176f.; "Papias," p. 339f.; "Date and Habitat of the Elders of Papias," p. 187; "John and the Pseudo-Johns," pp. 132f., 138f., 144, 149; "The Authoress of Revelation," pp. 235, 240, 244ff., 248f.; "The Mythical 'Elder John' of Ephesus," pp. 320, 323; "Johannes Redivivus," pp. 224, 226, 228f., 233f., 238, 241; "The Martyr Apostles," pp. 236f., 249f., 252; "Aristion," p. 116; "The Motivation of John 21:15-25," p. 79; "The Latin Prologues of John," p. 216f.; "Adhuc in Corpore Constituto," p. 305f.; *Studies in Matthew*, pp. 452ff., 463; *An Introduction to the New Testament,* pp. vi, 231f., 238, 275; *The Fourth Gospel in Research and Debate,* pp. 178, 181f.; *The Making of the New Testament,* p. 199. Such involutions, twists and turnings could only evoke a chorus of criticism; cf. William P. Armstrong, review of *The Fourth Gospel in Research and Debate, The Princeton Theological Review,* VIII (1910), pp. 312ff.; James Moffatt, review of *The Fourth Gospel in Research and Debate, The American Journal of Theology,* XIV (1910), p. 452f.; Clemen, p. 294f.; Meyer, p. 284f.; Lagrange, review of *The Fourth Gospel in Research and Debate,* pp. 138ff., and Goguel, pp. 417ff.

127. P. 61 above.

128. Cf. p. 25 above.

129. Cf. p. 24 above.

130. Cf. *Studies in Matthew*, p. 186.

131. Cf. p. 47f. above; "John as Preacher of Justification by Faith," p. 188; *Jesus The Son Of God or Primitive Christology*, pp. 91,100.

132. Cf. p. 64 above.

133. Cf. p. 63 above.

134. Cf. p. 80 above.

135. Cf. p. 24 above; "Reflections of Ritual in Paul," p. 524.

136. Cf. pp. 24 and 32 above.

137. Cf. p. 79 above.

138. Cf. p. 81 above, n. 82.

139. Cf. pp. 93f., 104.

140. Cf. "The Mythical Collapse of Historical Christianity," pp. 739, 741, 749.

141. Cf. p. 72 above.

142. For example, Moffatt's statement to the effect that Bacon had overthrown the tradition concerning Mark's Gospel as resting on Peter's discourses, reflects confusion regarding what Bacon assigned to the original Gospel and what to its final redactor. Cf. Moffatt, "B. W. Bacon, The Beginnings of Gospel Story," p. 227. In response to Bacon's statement that no special regard for Peter is to be found in Mark, Burkitt asked why a narrative founded on the Petrine reminiscences should show such regard. Here again, what Bacon had put asunder was joined, and the work of Mark confused with that of the final redactor. Cf. Burkitt, p. 89f. Similar charges were levelled at Bacon's Johannine studies. Hoskyns, e.g., faulted Bacon for driving a wedge between the Synoptists and the Fourth Evangelist, a judgement reflecting the failure to distinguish what Bacon believed derived from Servant-Wisdom tradition and what he thought rooted in Pauline or pre-Pauline, Hellenistic faith. Cf. Hoskyns, *The Fourth Gospel*, p. 37; cf. also Goguel, pp. 425, 430ff.

143. Buchanan, review of *Is Mark a Roman Gospel?* p. 116.

144. D. C. Macintosh, p. 430.

145. H. J. Holtzmann, review of *An Introduction to the New Testament, Theologische Literaturzeitung,* XXVI (1901), p. 321.

146. Cf. Moffatt, "Professor B. W. Bacon," p. 441.

147. Cadbury, review of *The Gospel of Mark,* p. 331.

148. A. J. Grieve, p. 88.

149. Enslin, p. 89.

150. Riddle, p. 470.

151. From the unpublished notes of Frank Chamberlain Porter.

152. Ernest William Parsons, "Professor Bacon's Studies in Matthew," *The Journal of Religion,* XI (1931), p. 283; de Bruyne thought the distinction between "S" and "Q" a mere matter of nomenclature; cf. Dom de Bruyne, review of *Studies in Matthew, Revue Benedictine,* XXXIV (1931), p. 75.

153. Taylor, p. 574.

154. Parsons, p. 283.

155. Cf. p. 90f. above.
156. Cf. "The Positivity Of The Christian Religion," *On Christianity, Early Theological Writings* by Friedrich Hegel, trans. T. M. Knox (New York: Harper Torchbooks, 1948), *passim;* Findlay, pp. 101, 132, and Mure, pp. 44f., 180f.
157. Cf. Findlay, p. 21.
158. *Ibid.,* pp. 142, 354. "It was in the course of his wanderings in the neighborhood of Golgotha and Gethsemane, rather than in his sojourn in Athenian gardens and colonnades, that Hegel first met 'the Idea'," *ibid.,* p. 133.
159. Cf. p. 44f. above.
160. Cf. "New Testament Science as a Historical Discipline," p. 91.
161. Cf. pp. 12 and 102 above.
162. Cf. *The Spectator,* p. 445; J. Gresham Machen, review of *A Commentary on The Epistle of Paul to the Galatians, The Princeton Theological Review,* IX(1911), p. 496. On the other hand, cf. H. A. A. Kennedy, review of *The Story of St. Paul, The American Journal of Theology,* IX (1905), p. 544.
163. The reader will recall Bacon's distinguishing two Jerusalem conclaves in Acts, the first reflected in chapters 11 and 12, the second in chapter 15; cf. p. 21f. above.
164. Cf. Findlay, p. 139. "What Hegel thinks important is not the *Incarnatio Filii Dei,* but the *belief* in such an incarnation: if this incarnation is said to be actual and not imaginary, its actuality is one *in* the believer, rather than in the historical person of Jesus. That person was no doubt the vehicle through which 'Absolute Religion', the realization that the divine nature must achieve self-consciousness in man, first became explicit: the realization rather than the vehicle remains the important thing for Hegel. Hegel may therefore fitly be regarded as the father of 'modernism', that ever assailed but unsuppressible and authentic expression of Christian belief." To the degree Bacon pressed home this aspect of the "gospel about Jesus," to that degree he was liable to the charge of "modernism."
165. Machen, review of *Is Mark a Roman Gospel?* p. 327.
166. H. A. A. Kennedy, p. 545.
167. Moffatt, review of *The Fourth Gospel in Research and Debate,* p.453.
168. Moulton, p. 433f.
169. Cf. Hoskyns, *The Fourth Gospel,* p. 38, and Macintosh, p. 430.
170. Moffatt, "Professor B. W. Bacon," p. 439.
171. "Was vorhanden ist muss notwendig im Begriffe gehalten seyn," cf. Findlay, p. 277.
172. Cf. p. 24f. above.
173. Cf. pp. 23 and 32 above.
174. Cf. p. 27 above.
175. Cf. p. 40 above.
176. Moffatt, "B. W. Bacon, The Beginnings of Gospel Story," p. 227.
177. Burkitt, p. 52.

178. Machen, review of *Is Mark a Roman Gospel?* p. 327.
179. Vincent Taylor, *The Gospel According To St. Mark* (London: The Macmillan Co., 1955), p. 129.
180. Cf. p. 63 above. Hegel wrote: "In John. . .we see the beginning of a profounder view: the deepest thought is wedded to the figure of the Christ, to the historical and external. . . ." *Philosophie Der Geschichte,* p. 456.
181. Cf. p. 67 above.
182. Cf. p. 10f. above.
183. Cf. p. 66 above.
184. Findlay, pp. 38, 47, 252.
185. *Ibid.,* p. 37.
186. Findlay writes: "It is plain, in fact, that Hegel's philosophical aim is not to *do* the work of history or science, nor to add to their results, but to frame concepts in terms of which these results can be philosophically grasped . . . . The dialectical method . . . involves no personal pushing or interference: the dialectician, like some quietist saint, must simply wait upon, or surrender himself to the 'immanent rhythm' of his notions," *ibid.,* pp. 24, 66.
187. Cf. Mure, p. 37, n. 1.
188. "The notion . . . is that of the contingent and arbitrary which is, in a sense, divested of arbitrariness and contingency by being shown to be a necessary condition of what is universal and rational. The rational, universal Will *requires* a body of contingent material purposes which it can organize and unify. . . . These contingent purposes are . . . . taken up, or done away with, in the overriding rationality of which they furnish the presupposition," Findlay, p. 307.
189. In other words, God=the universality and unity in all thinking=the finite, particular self=the self-conscious "I." Hegel wrote: "The absolute object, the truth, is Spirit, and because man himself is Spirit, he is present to himself in this object, and thus in his absolute object has found essential being (*Wesen*) and his own essential being. . . . The human and divine nature . . . are one, and man, insofar as he is Spirit, has the essentiality and substantiality which adheres to the idea of God. . . . Man must seek in himself for that contingent (*das Dieses*) which is divine," *Philosophie Der Geschichte,* pp. 440, 512, 532.
190. Cf. Findlay, p. 248.
191. "The union of human and divine is not adequately symbolized by miraculous attributes which are no longer intellectually tolerable," Mure, p. 49.
192. Cf. p. 9 above.
193. Cf. p. 74f. above. Note also Bacon's refusal to describe Jesus as employing the Son of Man title as self-designation, p. 78 above.
194. Cf. pp. 26, 38, 42 above.

195. Cf. Burkitt, p. 57; *The Times Literary Supplement,* p. 20; E. F. Scott,
     p. 155; Cadbury, review of *The Gospel of Mark,* p. 330; Lagrange,
     review of *The Gospel of Mark,* p. 313f.; Buchanan, review of *The
     Gospel of Mark,* p. 51f.; Taylor, review of *Studies in Matthew,* p. 576;
     G. R. Beasley-Murray, *A Commentary On Mark Thirteen* (London:
     The Macmillan Co., 1957), p. 65f.; Albert Schweitzer, p. 586. Of
     Bacon's method and conclusions Lagrange could only exclaim:
     "Renversant une casserole, il s'en servait comme d'une table pour
     immoler des oiseaux," review of *The Gospel of Mark,* p. 314.
196. Cf. *The Triple Tradition of the Exodus, passim.*
197. "Ultimate Problems of Biblical Science," p.11.
198. "A purely formal view of development as such can neither give
     preference to the one or other mode, nor make clear the purpose of
     that decay in earlier stages of development. Rather, it must view such
     events, and particularly their decline, as external contingencies, and
     can assign priorities only from an indeterminate point of view. Since
     the development as such is all that matters, these points of view are
     relative and not absolute aims." In the ultimate, of course, Spirit
     comes forth from its decay "exalted, transfigured, a purer Spirit," thus
     rendering its decline an "external contingency," Hegel, *Philosophie
     Der Geschichte,* pp. 108, 130.
199. Cf. *The Triple Tradition of the Exodus, passim.*
200. Cf. p. 9 above.
201. "The attestation of Christ's divinity is the witness of one's own spirit,
     not miracles; for only Spirit recognizes Spirit. . . . Miracle means
     that the natural course of things is interrupted; but what a man calls
     the natural course is very much a relative thing, and by this definition
     the force of a magnet is a miracle. . . . It was less the apostles'
     miracles gave Christianity this outer extension and inner strength than
     the content, the truth of the doctrine itself," Hegel, *Philosophie Der
     Geschichte,* pp. 448, 452.
202. Cf. p. 39 above.
203. Cf. *Jesus and Paul,* pp. 167ff.; "'The Resurrection' in Byzantine Art,"
     pp. 29, 31, 35; "The Resurrection in Primitive Tradition and
     Observance," p. 396. Cf. also p. 81 above.
204. Cf. p. 25f. above.
205. Cf. p. 76 above.
206. Cf. p. 25 above.   Hegel wrote: "In his death and in his story as a
     whole, Christ, the man as such in whom appeared the unity of God and
     man, portrayed the eternal history of Spirit — a history which every
     man must achieve himself, in order to be Spirit or child of God, citizen
     of his Kingdom," *Philosophie Der Geschichte,* p. 451f.
207. "The Christian religion . . . has one foot in the present tense of self-
     consciousness," *ibid.,* p. 527.
208. Recall the "Hegelian" remark on p. 10 above: "The man that is to
     be. . .is the revealer, the Logos of God."

209. Cf. Roy A. Harrisville, *Frank Chamberlain Porter: Pioneer In American Biblical Interpretation* (Missoula, Scholars Press, 1976), Chap. 3.
210. Cf. p. 9f. above.
211. For Hegel, law was part of things as they are, and in it the Spirit was merely implicit. Thought, however, demanded that the "ideal" should take the place of things as they are, and thus spell their rupture or corruption. Cf. *Philosophie Der Geschichte,* pp. 375f., 402. Hegel concluded his discussion of the corruption of the Athenian status quo as follows: "When Socrates is sentenced to death because he voices the principle which must now emerge, there is lofty justice in the Athenians' sentencing their deadly enemy. But there is also high tragedy in their being forced to discover that what they condemned in Socrates had already taken firm root in them, and that they must be charged or acquitted with him. In this mood they condemned Socrates' accusers and declared him innocent," *ibid.,* p. 379. Similarly, the Gracchi symbolized thought's transgression of things as they are, a transgression which also had the "higher sanction of the World-Spirit," *ibid.,* p. 430. On Hegel's view of law as connected with abstract, i.e. unreflective, undeveloped thought (*Denken, Verstand*), cf. his discussion of the French revolution in *ibid.,* pp. 589ff.
212. Cf. Mackay, pp. 300, 303; Machen, review of *Commentary on The Epistle of Paul to the Galatians,* p. 497, and of *He Opened To Us The Scriptures,* p. 641f.
213. "This conviction and insight is an assumption in the area of history as such; in philosophy it is no assumption," Hegel, *Philosophie Der Geschichte,* p. 49.
214. Cf. Findlay, p. 140.
215. Cf. Mure, p. 44.
216. Recall the equation in note 189 above.
217. Cf. Theodor Litt's "Einführung" to Hegel's *Philosophie Der Geschichte,* pp. 4ff.
218. Bacon's nomenclature here is strikingly reminiscent of Hegel's discussion of the second type of reflective history, viz., the "pragmatical," whose purpose is to "quicken the annals of the past with life," *Philosophie Der Geschichte,* p. 45.
219. Cf. C. J. Friedrichs' Introduction to Hegel, *The Philosophy of History,* trans. J. Sibree (New York: Dover Publications, 1956), p. i., and *Philosophie Der Geschichte,* p. 605.
220. Hegel, *Philosophie Der Geschichte,* p. 478f.
221. *Ibid.,* p. 584.
222. Cf. Findlay, p. 209.
223. "Ultimate Problems of Biblical Science," p. 9.
224. "The Supernatural Birth of Jesus," p. 1.
225. *The Apostolic Message,* p. 44.
226. "Ultimate Problems of Biblical Science," p. 3f.

227. "The 'Deficiencies' of Christ's Sufferings," *The Church Union,* XXV
     (1898), pp. 362ff.
228. "Royce's Interpretation of Christianity," p. 328.
229. Cf. p. 13 above.
230. Hegel's term was *Innerlichkeit.*
231. Cf. Bacon's interpretation of Jesus' self-consciousness; his unity with
     the Father; temptations; preaching of the Kingdom; his death and the
     apocalyptic background of his consciousness and mission, pp. 72f.,
     76f., 79f. above, "Each," wrote Hegel, "must complete the work
     of reconciliation in himself," *Philosophie Der Geschichte,* p. 558.
232. Hegel, *Philosophie Der Geschichte,* p. 584; cf. p. 593.
233. Machen, review of *Jesus and Paul,* p. 686.
234. I.e., in Paul's struggle with Judaism; cf. p. 26 above.

A BACON BIBLIOGRAPHY
Listing titles not included in the footnotes

"Observance of Sunday, A Plea for the Civil Sabbath," *The New Haven Sunday Register,* July 3, 1881.

"The Propagation Of The Gospel Along The Lines Of Kindred And Friendship," *The Homiletic Review,* X, 1885.

"Beautifying The House of the Lord," a sermon Preached in Old Lyme Congregational Church, on occasion of Improvements being Proposed on the Building, Sunday, September 12, 1886.

"Is Theology Scientific?" *The New Englander,* X, 1887.

"Use and Abuse of Creed," *The Silent Worker,* December, 1889.

"JE in the Middle Books of the Pentateuch. II. Analysis of Exodus i.-vii," *Hebraica,* VII, 1891.

"The Victory That Overcometh the World," *The Christian Register,* September 17, 1891.

"The Two Gardens," *The Sunday School Times,* XXIV, 1892.

Review of *Die Genesis* by August Dillmann, *The New World,* II, 1893.

"The Consensus of Scholarship on the Pentateuch Question," *The Independent,* XLVI, 1894.

"A Study of the Hexateuch," *The Independent,* XLVI, 1894.

"The Historical David," *The New World,* IV, 1895.

"The Genealogy of Jesus," *The Expository Times,* VIII, 1897.

"The New Sayings of Jesus," *The Independent,* XLIX, 1897.

"The Problem of Church Attendance," *The Independent,* L, 1898.

"A Criticism of the New Chronology of Paul," *The Expositor,* VII, 1898.

"A Criticism of the New Chronology of Paul II," *The Expositor,* X, 1899.

"Professor Ramsay on the Incidence of Passover and the Use of German Authorities," *The Expositor,* II, 1900.

Review of *Das Johannesevangelium* by Hans Heinrich Wendt; *Christianity in the Apostolic Age* by George T. Purves; *Ten Epochs of Church History* by James Vernon Bartlet, *The American Journal of Theology* V. 1901.

Review of *Authenticite et date des livres du Nouveau Testament* by Gustave Desjardins; *Untersuchungen über die Entstehung des Vierten Evangeliums* by Julius Grill; *Das Evangelium der Wahrheit* by Johannes Kreyenbühl; *The Earliest Gospel* by Allan Menzies; *Unsere Evangelien, ihre Quellen und ihr Quellenwerth* by Wilhelm Soltau, *The American Journal of Theology,* VI, 1902.

Review of *Die urchristlichen Gemeinden: Sittengeschichtliche Bilder* by Ernst von Dobschütz, *The Biblical World,* XX, 1902.

"The Canon of the New Testament," *The Biblical World,* XXI, 1903.

"Recent Aspects of the Johannine Problem: II. Direct Internal Evidence," *The Hibbert Journal,* II, 1904.

"The Use of Creeds in Worship," *Yale Divinity Quarterly,* I, 1904.

"Studies in Bible Themes," *The Homiletic Review,* XLVIII, 1904.

"The Student Y.M.C.A. as seen from the Viewpoint of Faculty Men," *Yale Divinity Quarterly,* V, 1908.

"Aenon Near to Salim," *The Biblical World,* XXXIII, 1909.

"The Ascension in Luke and Acts," *The Expositor,* VII, 1909.

Introduction to Ora Delmer Foster, "The Literary Relations of 'The First Epistle of Peter'," *Transactions of the Connecticut Academy of Arts and Sciences,* XVII, New Haven: Yale University Press, 1913.

"Will the Son of Man Find Faith on the Earth?" *The Expositor,* VIII, 1914.

"The 'Single' Eye," *The Expositor,* VII, 1914.

"The Yale University School of Religion," appended to Anson Phelps Stokes' "University Schools of Religion," an address delivered by Stokes before the National Religious Education Association, March 6, 1914.

"The Christ-Party in Corinth," *The Expositor,* VIII, 1914.

"Again the Ephesian Imprisonment of Paul," *The Expositor,* IX, 1915.

"Yale in Divinity," *The Book of the Yale Pageant, 21 October 1916.* In Commemoration of the Two Hundredth Anniversary of the Removal of Yale College to New Haven, ed. George Henry Nettleton, New Haven: Yale University Press, 1916.

"The Call of the Present Situation to International Protestantism," an address at the Mayflower Tercentenary, Plymouth, England, September 6, 1920, *The Christian World Pulpit,* XCVIII, 1920.

"Ten Critical Years," *Yale Divinity News,* XVII, 1920.

"Jesus' 'Native Place' in John," *The Expositor,* XXIII, 1922.

"A Congregational Leader," *The Congregationalist,* CVII, 1922.

"Parable and Its Adaptation in the Gospels," *The Hibbert Journal,* XXI, 1922.

"Lux et Veritas," a hymn written for the Centennial of the Yale Divinity School, 1822 - 1922, *Yale Alumni Weekly,* October 20, 1922.

"The Reading οἷζ οὐδέ In Gal. 2:5," *Journal of Biblical Literature*, XLII, 1923.

"A Devoted Teacher," an essay on the retirement of Frank Chamberlain Porter, *Yale Divinity News,* XXIII, 1927.